ISBN: 9798636103585

Contents

STUFFED PEPPERONCINI

Servings: 36 | Prep: 45m | Cooks: 1h | Total: 1h45m

NUTRITION FACTS

Calories: 52 | Carbohydrates: 1.9g | Fat: 4.4g | Protein: 1.3g | Cholesterol: 10mg

INGREDIENTS

- 6 slices bacon, cut into small pieces
- 1/3 cup minced shallots
- 1 red bell pepper, minced
- 1 (8 ounce) package cream cheese, softened
- 1 tablespoon milk
- 32 ounces pepperoncini

DIRECTIONS

1. In a large skillet, cook bacon over medium heat until bacon is browned. Move bacon to paper towels. Keep bacon drippings.
2. In drippings, cook shallots and red pepper over medium heat until vegetables are tender. Cook about 5 minutes. Remove skillet from heat and let cool for 20 minutes.
3. In a small bowl, beat cream cheese and milk with an electric mixer at medium speed until smooth. Stir bacon and shallot into the mixture.
4. Spoon cream cheese mixture into a heavy weight plastic bag. Cut a small hole in one corner to squeeze the filling from. With small knife, cut a slit lengthwise into each pepper. Do not cut the whole way through the pepper. By squeezing the bag, pipe cream cheese mixture into peppers. Cover and refrigerate for at least 1 hour, up to one day.

AIR FRYER STUFFED MUSHROOMS

Servings: 6 | Prep: 20m | Cooks: 10m | Total: 35m

NUTRITION FACTS

Calories: 103 | Carbohydrates: 3.5g | Fat: 8.4g | Protein: 5g | Cholesterol: 26mg

INGREDIENTS

- 1 (16 ounce) package whole white button mushrooms
- 2 scallions
- 1 pinch salt
- 1/4 cup finely shredded sharp Cheddar cheese
- 1/4 teaspoon ground paprika
- cooking spray

- 4 ounces cream cheese, softened

DIRECTIONS

1. Using a damp cloth, gently clean mushrooms. Remove stems and discard.
2. Mince scallions and separate white and green parts.
3. Preheat an air fryer to 360 degrees F (182 degrees C).
4. Combine cream cheese, Cheddar cheese, the white parts from the scallions, paprika, and salt in a small bowl. Stuff filling into the mushrooms, pressing it in to fill the cavity with the back of a small spoon.
5. Spray the air fryer basket with cooking spray and set mushrooms inside. Depending on the size of your air fryer, you may have to do 2 batches.
6. Cook mushrooms until filling is lightly browned, about 8 minutes. Repeat with remaining mushrooms.
7. Sprinkle mushrooms with scallion greens and let cool for 5 minutes before serving.

EVERYTHING DEVILED EGGS
Servings: 12 | Prep: 15m | Cooks: 20m | Total: 35m

NUTRITION FACTS

Calories: 40 | Carbohydrates: 0.4g | Fat: 2.7g | Protein: : 3.3g | Cholesterol: 93mg

INGREDIENTS

- 6 large eggs
- 2 tablespoons full-fat plain Greek yogurt
- 1 teaspoon prepared yellow mustard
- 1/4 teaspoon everything bagel seasoning, or to taste
- 1 teaspoon white vinegar
- 1/2 teaspoon Worcestershire sauce
- 1/4 teaspoon white sugar
- 1 teaspoon sliced scallion greens

DIRECTIONS

1. Place eggs in a saucepan and cover with water. Bring to a boil, remove from heat, and let eggs stand in hot water for 15 minutes. Remove eggs from hot water, cool under cold running water, and peel.
2. Slice eggs in half lengthwise and set the whites aside. Place yolks in a mini blender or food processor; pulse several times until finely chopped. Add yogurt, mustard, vinegar, Worcestershire sauce, and sugar and blend until smooth.

3. Transfer yolk mixture to pastry bag fitted with a large star tip and pipe filling into the egg whites (or stuff filling into egg whites with a spoon). Sprinkle with everything bagel seasoning and garnish with sliced scallions. Chill in the refrigerator until ready serve.

EASY RUMAKI WITH PINEAPPLE
Servings: 24 | Prep: 20m | Cooks: 20m | Total: 40m | Servings: 24

NUTRITION FACTS

Calories: 40 | Carbohydrates: 3.7g | Fat: 2g | Protein: 1.7g | Cholesterol: 5mg

INGREDIENTS

- cooking spray
- 24 (1 inch) cubes fresh pineapple
- 24 water chestnut slices
- 8 thick-cut bacon slices, cut crosswise into 3 pieces
- 24 toothpicks
- 1/2 cup low-fat sesame-ginger salad dressing
- 1 tablespoon chopped green onion, or to taste

DIRECTIONS

1. Preheat oven to 375 degrees F (190 degrees C). Line the bottom section of a broiler pan with aluminum foil, top with the broiler rack, and spray rack with cooking spray.
2. Place a water chestnut slice atop each pineapple cube; wrap each with 1 bacon slice, securing with a toothpick. Arrange wrapped pineapple on the prepared broiler rack.
3. Bake in the preheated oven for 7 minutes; turn and continue baking until bacon is almost crisp, about 8 more minutes. Brush rumaki with sesame-ginger dressing and continue baking until bacon is crisp, about 5 more minutes. Garnish rumaki with green onion.

FRIED MOZZARELLA PUFFS
Servings: 6 | Prep: 20m | Cooks: 15m | Total: 1h40m

NUTRITION FACTS

Calories: 289 | Carbohydrates: 12.1g | Fat: 23.7g | Protein: 7.4g | Cholesterol: 55mg

INGREDIENTS

- 1/3 cup water
- 2 tablespoons unsalted butter
- 1 pinch freshly ground black pepper
- 1/2 teaspoon dried oregano

- 1 teaspoon kosher salt
- 1/3 cup all-purpose flour
- 1 large egg
- 1 pinch cayenne pepper
- 1 anchovy fillet

- 1 cup marinara sauce, or to taste
- 1/2 teaspoon red pepper flakes
- 1 teaspoon balsamic vinegar
- 4 cups canola oil for frying

DIRECTIONS

1. Combine water, butter, and salt in a saucepan over medium-high heat. Bring to a simmer; pour in flour all at once and reduce heat to medium. Stir with a wooden spoon or spatula until a dough starts coming together. Cook, scraping up and stirring the dough, for 2 to 3 minutes.
2. Remove from heat; transfer dough to a mixing bowl. Let cool until no longer hot but still very warm, 5 to 10 minutes. Add egg and season with cayenne and freshly ground black pepper. Whisk vigorously until mixture combines into a very soft, sticky dough. Switch to a spatula and scrape dough into a ball.
3. Seal dough and spatula with plastic wrap and refrigerate in the bowl until cool, about 1 hour.
4. In the meantime, season marinara sauce with oregano, red pepper flakes, balsamic vinegar in a small pot over medium heat. Add anchovy fillet. Stir together and bring to a simmer. Let simmer for 10 minutes; turn off heat and let sit until ready to use.
5. Grate mozzarella cheese over the dough and stir to combine.
6. Heat oil to 350 degrees F (175 degrees C) in a deep fryer or heavy-duty pan over medium heat. Preheat oven to 200 degrees F (93 degrees C) or any temperature for keeping warm.
7. Scoop out about 2 tablespoons of dough per puff and form into a football shape using two spoons. Fry puffs, 5 or 6 at a time, in the hot oil until browned, 2 to 3 minutes. Drain on paper towels. Keep puffs warm in low oven while frying the rest. Serve with hot marinara sauce.

STRAWBERRY BRUSCHETTA

Servings: 12 | Prep: 10m | Cooks: 5m | Total: 15m

NUTRITION FACTS

Calories: 120 | Carbohydrates: 23.1g | Fat: 1.6g | Protein: 3.7g | Cholesterol: 3mg

INGREDIENTS

- 24 slices French baguette
- 1 tablespoon butter, softened

- 2 cups chopped fresh strawberries
- 1/4 cup white sugar, or as needed

DIRECTIONS

1. Preheat your oven's broiler. Spread a thin layer of butter on each slice of bread. Arrange bread slices in a single layer on a large baking sheet.

2. Place bread under the broiler for 1 to 2 minutes, just until lightly toasted. Spoon some chopped strawberries onto each piece of toast, then sprinkle sugar over the strawberries.

3. Place under the broiler again until sugar is caramelized, 3 to 5 minutes. Serve immediately.

GARLICKY APPETIZER SHRIMP SCAMPI
Servings: 6 | Prep: 15m | Cooks: 6m | Total: 21m

NUTRITION FACTS

Calories: 302 | Carbohydrates: 0.9g | Fat: 21.8g | Protein: 25g | Cholesterol: 261mg

INGREDIENTS

- 6 tablespoons unsalted butter, softened
- 1/4 cup olive oil
- 1 tablespoon minced garlic
- 1 tablespoon minced shallots
- 2 tablespoons minced fresh chives
- salt and freshly ground black pepper to taste
- 1/2 teaspoon paprika
- 2 pounds large shrimp - peeled and deveined

DIRECTIONS

1. Preheat grill for high heat.

2. In a large bowl, mix together softened butter, olive oil, garlic, shallots, chives, salt, pepper, and paprika; add the shrimp, and toss to coat.

3. Lightly oil grill grate. Cook the shrimp as close to the flame as possible for 2 to 3 minutes per side, or until opaque.

ARTICHOKE HEARTS GRATIN
Servings: 4 | Prep: 10m | Cooks: 10m | Total: 35m

NUTRITION FACTS

Calories: 89 | Carbohydrates: 6.3g | Fat: 6.2g | Protein: 3.3g | Cholesterol: 4mg

INGREDIENTS

- 6 canned artichoke hearts, drained and halved
- 1 teaspoon vegetable oil
- salt and freshly ground black pepper to taste
- 2 tablespoons dry bread crumbs
- 1/4 cup finely grated Parmigiano-Reggiano cheese
- 1 tablespoon olive oil
- 1/2 lemon, cut into wedges

DIRECTIONS

1. Place artichoke heart halves on a paper towel cut-side down to drain for about 15 minutes.
2. Set oven rack about 6 inches from the heat source and preheat the oven's broiler. Line a baking sheet with aluminum foil and lightly coat with vegetable oil.
3. Place artichoke heart halves on the prepared baking sheet, cut side up. Season with salt and pepper, sprinkle with breadcrumbs and Parmigiano-Reggiano cheese, and drizzle with olive oil.
4. Broil artichoke hearts until browned on top, about 7 minutes. Serve with lemon wedges.

BUFFALO CHICKEN DIP

Servings: 20 | Prep: 5m | Cooks: 40m | Total: 45m

NUTRITION FACTS

- Calories: 284 | Carbohydrates: 8.6g | Fat: 22.6g | Protein: 11.1g | Cholesterol: 54mg

INGREDIENTS

- 2 (10 ounce) cans chunk chicken, drained
- 2 (8 ounce) packages cream cheese, softened
- 1 cup Ranch dressing
- 3/4 cup pepper sauce (such as Frank's Red Hot®)
- 1 1/2 cups shredded Cheddar cheese
- 1 bunch celery, cleaned and cut into 4 inch pieces
- 1 (8 ounce) box chicken-flavored crackers

DIRECTIONS

1. Heat chicken and hot sauce in a skillet over medium heat, until heated through. Stir in cream cheese and ranch dressing. Cook, stirring until well blended and warm. Mix in half of the shredded cheese, and transfer the mixture to a slow cooker. Sprinkle the remaining cheese over the top, cover, and cook on Low setting until hot and bubbly. Serve with celery sticks and crackers.

MOUTH-WATERING STUFFED MUSHROOMS
Servings: 12 | Prep: 25m | Cooks: 20m | Total: 45m

NUTRITION FACTS

Calories: 88 | Carbohydrates: 1.5g | Fat: 8.2g | Protein: 2.7g | Cholesterol: 22mg

INGREDIENTS

- 12 whole fresh mushrooms
- 1 tablespoon vegetable oil
- 1 tablespoon minced garlic
- 1 (8 ounce) package cream cheese, softened
- 1/4 cup grated Parmesan cheese
- 1/4 teaspoon ground black pepper
- 1/4 teaspoon onion powder
- 1/4 teaspoon ground cayenne pepper

DIRECTIONS

1. Preheat oven to 350 degrees F (175 degrees C). Spray a baking sheet with cooking spray. Clean mushrooms with a damp paper towel. Carefully break off stems. Chop stems extremely fine, discarding tough end of stems.
2. Heat oil in a large skillet over medium heat. Add garlic and chopped mushroom stems to the skillet. Fry until any moisture has disappeared, taking care not to burn garlic. Set aside to cool.
3. When garlic and mushroom mixture is no longer hot, stir in cream cheese, Parmesan cheese, black pepper, onion powder and cayenne pepper. Mixture should be very thick. Using a little spoon, fill each mushroom cap with a generous amount of stuffing. Arrange the mushroom caps on prepared cookie sheet.
4. Bake for 20 minutes in the preheated oven, or until the mushrooms are piping hot and liquid starts to form under caps.

RESTAURANT-STYLE BUFFALO CHICKEN WINGS
Servings: 5 | Prep: 15m | Cooks: 15m | Total: 2h | Additional: 1h30m

NUTRITION FACTS

Calories: 364 | Carbohydrates: 10.7g | Fat: 32.4g | Protein: 7.9g | Cholesterol: 44mg

INGREDIENTS

- 1/2 cup all-purpose flour
- 1/4 teaspoon paprika
- oil for deep frying
- 1/4 cup butter

- 1/4 teaspoon cayenne pepper
- 1/4 teaspoon salt
- 10 chicken wings
- 1/4 cup hot sauce
- 1 dash ground black pepper
- 1 dash garlic powder

DIRECTIONS

1. In a small bowl mix together the flour, paprika, cayenne pepper and salt. Place chicken wings in a large nonporous glass dish or bowl and sprinkle flour mixture over them until they are evenly coated. Cover dish or bowl and refrigerate for 60 to 90 minutes.
2. Heat oil in a deep fryer to 375 degrees F (190 degrees C). The oil should be just enough to cover wings entirely, an inch or so deep. Combine the butter, hot sauce, pepper and garlic powder in a small saucepan over low heat. Stir together and heat until butter is melted and mixture is well blended. Remove from heat and reserve for serving.
3. Fry coated wings in hot oil for 10 to 15 minutes, or until parts of wings begin to turn brown. Remove from heat, place wings in serving bowl, add hot sauce mixture and stir together. Serve.

DOUBLE TOMATO BRUSCHETTA
Servings: 12 | Prep: 15m | Cooks: 7m | Total: 35m

NUTRITION FACTS

Calories: 215 | Carbohydrates: 24.8g | Fat: 8.9g | Protein: 9.6g | Cholesterol: 12mg

INGREDIENTS

- 6 roma (plum) tomatoes, chopped
- 1/2 cup sun-dried tomatoes, packed in oil
- 3 cloves minced garlic
- 1/4 cup olive oil
- 2 tablespoons balsamic vinegar
- 1/4 cup fresh basil, stems removed
- 1/4 teaspoon salt
- 1/4 teaspoon ground black pepper
- 1 French baguette
- 2 cups shredded mozzarella cheese

DIRECTIONS

1. Preheat the oven on broiler setting.
2. In a large bowl, combine the roma tomatoes, sun-dried tomatoes, garlic, olive oil, vinegar, basil, salt, and pepper. Allow the mixture to sit for 10 minutes.

3. Cut the baguette into 3/4-inch slices. On a baking sheet, arrange the baguette slices in a single layer. Broil for 1 to 2 minutes, until slightly brown.

4. Divide the tomato mixture evenly over the baguette slices. Top the slices with mozzarella cheese.

5. Broil for 5 minutes, or until the cheese is melted.

ASIAN LETTUCE WRAPS

Servings: 4 | Prep: 20m | Cooks: 15m | Total: 35m

NUTRITION FACTS

Calories: 388 | Carbohydrates: 24.3g | Fat: 22.3g | Protein: 23.4g | Cholesterol: 69mg

INGREDIENTS

- 16 Boston Bibb or butter lettuce leaves
- 1 pound lean ground beef
- 1 tablespoon cooking oil
- 1 large onion, chopped
- 1/4 cup hoisin sauce
- 2 cloves fresh garlic, minced
- 1 tablespoon soy sauce
- 1 tablespoon rice wine vinegar
- 2 teaspoons minced pickled ginger
- 1 dash Asian chile pepper sauce, or to taste (optional)
- 1 (8 ounce) can water chestnuts, drained and finely chopped
- 1 bunch green onions, chopped
- 2 teaspoons Asian (dark) sesame oil

DIRECTIONS

1. Rinse whole lettuce leaves and pat dry, being careful not tear them. Set aside.
2. Heat a large skillet over medium-high heat. Cook and stir beef and cooking oil in the hot skillet until browned and crumbly, 5 to 7 minutes. Drain and discard grease; transfer beef to a bowl. Cook and stir onion in the same skillet used for beef until slightly tender, 5 to 10 minutes. Stir hoisin sauce, garlic, soy sauce, vinegar, ginger, and chile pepper sauce into onions. Add water chestnuts, green onions, sesame oil, and cooked beef; cook and stir until the onions just begin to wilt, about 2 minutes.
3. Arrange lettuce leaves around the outer edge of a large serving platter and pile meat mixture in the center.

BROWN SUGAR SMOKIES

Servings: 12 | Prep: 10m | Cooks: 20m | Total: 30m

NUTRITION FACTS

Calories: 356 | Carbohydrates: 18.9g | Fat: 27.2g | Protein: 9g | Cholesterol: 49mg

INGREDIENTS

- 1 pound bacon
- 1 cup brown sugar, or to taste

- 1 (16 ounce) package little smokie sausages

DIRECTIONS

1. Preheat oven to 350 degrees F (175 degrees C).
2. Cut bacon into thirds and wrap each strip around a little sausage. Place the wrapped sausages on wooden skewers, several to a skewer. Arrange the skewers on a baking sheet and sprinkle them liberally with brown sugar.
3. Bake until bacon is crisp and the brown sugar melted.

COCONUT SHRIMP
Servings: 6 | Prep: 10m | Cooks: 20m | Total: 1h

NUTRITION FACTS

Calories: 317 | Carbohydrates: 26.3g | Fat: 19.3g | Protein: 8.4g | Cholesterol: 67mg

INGREDIENTS

- 1 egg
- 1/2 cup all-purpose flour
- 2/3 cup beer
- 1 1/2 teaspoons baking powder
- 2 cups flaked coconut
- 24 shrimp
- 3 cups oil for frying

  1/4 cup all-purpose flour

DIRECTIONS

1. In medium bowl, combine egg, 1/2 cup flour, beer and baking powder. Place 1/4 cup flour and coconut in two separate bowls.
2. Hold shrimp by tail, and dredge in flour, shaking off excess flour. Dip in egg/beer batter; allow excess to drip off. Roll shrimp in coconut, and place on a baking sheet lined with wax paper. Refrigerate for 30 minutes. Meanwhile, heat oil to 350 degrees F (175 degrees C) in a deep-fryer.
3. Fry shrimp in batches: cook, turning once, for 2 to 3 minutes, or until golden brown. Using tongs, remove shrimp to paper towels to drain. Serve warm with your favorite dipping sauce.

COCKTAIL MEATBALLS
Servings: 10 | Prep: 20m | Cooks: 1h25m | Total: 1h45m

NUTRITION FACTS

Calories: 193 | Carbohydrates: 15.2g | Fat: 10.2g | Protein: 9.8g | Cholesterol: 53mg

INGREDIENTS

- 1 pound lean ground beef
- 1 egg
- 2 tablespoons water
- 1/2 cup bread crumbs
- 3 tablespoons minced onion

- 1 (8 ounce) can jellied cranberry sauce
- 3/4 cup chili sauce
- 1 tablespoon brown sugar
- 1 1/2 teaspoons lemon juice

DIRECTIONS

1. Preheat oven to 350 degrees F (175 degrees C).
2. In a large bowl, mix together the ground beef, egg, water, bread crumbs, and minced onion. Roll into small meatballs.
3. Bake in preheated oven for 20 to 25 minutes, turning once.
4. In a slow cooker or large saucepan over low heat, blend the cranberry sauce, chili sauce, brown sugar, and lemon juice. Add meatballs, and simmer for 1 hour before serving.

PLAYGROUP GRANOLA BARS
Servings: 24 | Prep: 15m | Cooks: 35m | Total: 50m

NUTRITION FACTS

Calories: 161 | Carbohydrates: 26.6g | Fat: 5.5g | Protein: 2.4g | Cholesterol: 8mg

INGREDIENTS

- 2 cups rolled oats
- 3/4 cup packed brown sugar
- 3/4 cup raisins (optional)
- 1/2 cup honey
- 1/2 cup vegetable oil
- 1/2 cup wheat germ

- 3/4 teaspoon ground cinnamon
- 1 cup all-purpose flour
- 3/4 teaspoon salt
- 1 egg, beaten
- 2 teaspoons vanilla extract

DIRECTIONS

1. Preheat the oven to 350 degrees F (175 degrees C). Generously grease a 9x13 inch baking pan.
2. In a large bowl, mix together the oats, brown sugar, wheat germ, cinnamon, flour, raisins and salt. Make a well in the center, and pour in the honey, egg, oil and vanilla. Mix well using your hands. Pat the mixture evenly into the prepared pan.
3. Bake for 30 to 35 minutes in the preheated oven, until the bars begin to turn golden at the edges. Cool for 5 minutes, then cut into bars while still warm. Do not allow the bars to cool completely before cutting, or they will be too hard to cut.

BACON WRAPPED SMOKIES
Servings: 16 | Prep: 45m | Cooks: 45m | Total: 1h30m

NUTRITION FACTS

Calories: 163 | Carbohydrates: 10.7g | Fat: 10.5g | Protein: 6.5g | Cholesterol: 26mg

INGREDIENTS

- 1 pound sliced bacon, cut into thirds
- 1 (14 ounce) package beef cocktail wieners
- 3/4 cup brown sugar, or to taste

DIRECTIONS

1. Preheat the oven to 325 degrees F (165 degrees C).
2. Refrigerate 2/3 of the bacon until needed. It is easier to wrap the wieners with cold bacon. Wrap each cocktail wiener with a piece of bacon and secure with a toothpick. Place on a large baking sheet. Sprinkle brown sugar generously over all.
3. Bake for 40 minutes in the preheated oven, until the sugar is bubbly. To serve, place the wieners in a slow cooker and keep on the low setting.

BACON CHEDDAR DEVILED EGGS
Servings: 12 | Prep: 30m | Cooks: 10m | Total: 40m

NUTRITION FACTS

Calories: 187 | Carbohydrates: 0.8g | Fat: 17g | Protein: 7.9g | Cholesterol: 197mg

INGREDIENTS

- 12 eggs
- 1/2 cup mayonnaise
- 4 slices bacon
- 2 tablespoons finely shredded Cheddar cheese
- 1 tablespoon mustard

DIRECTIONS

1. Place eggs in a saucepan, and cover with cold water. Bring water to a boil and immediately remove from heat. Cover, and let eggs stand in hot water for 10 to 12 minutes. Remove from hot water, and cool. To cool more quickly, rinse eggs under cold running water.
2. Meanwhile, place bacon in a large, deep skillet. Cook over medium-high heat until evenly brown. Alternatively, wrap bacon in paper towels and cook in the microwave for about 1 minute per slice. Crumble and set aside.
3. Peel the hard-cooked eggs, and cut in half lengthwise. Remove yolks to a small bowl. Mash egg yolks with mayonnaise, crumbled bacon and cheese. Stir in mustard. Fill egg white halves with the yolk mixture and refrigerate until serving.

BAKED BUFFALO WINGS

Servings: 20 | Prep: 15m | Cooks: 45m | Total: 2h | Additional: 1h

NUTRITION FACTS

Calories: 125 | Carbohydrates: 3.8g | Fat: 9.2g | Protein: 6.8g | Cholesterol: 32mg

INGREDIENTS

- 3/4 cup all-purpose flour
- 1/2 teaspoon cayenne pepper
- 1/2 teaspoon garlic powder
- 1/2 teaspoon salt
- 20 chicken wings
- 1/2 cup melted butter
- 1/2 cup hot pepper sauce

DIRECTIONS

1. Line a baking sheet with aluminum foil, and lightly grease with cooking spray. Place the flour, cayenne pepper, garlic powder, and salt into a resealable plastic bag, and shake to mix. Add the chicken wings, seal, and toss until well coated with the flour mixture. Place the wings onto the prepared baking sheet, and place into the refrigerator. Refrigerate at least 1 hour.
2. Preheat oven to 400 degrees F (200 degrees C).

3. Whisk together the melted butter and hot sauce in a small bowl. Dip the wings into the butter mixture, and place back on the baking sheet. Bake in the preheated oven until the chicken is no longer pink in the center, and crispy on the outside, about 45 minutes. Turn the wings over halfway during cooking so they cook evenly.

APANESE CHICKEN WINGS

Servings: 6 | Prep: 15m | Cooks: 45m | Total: 1h

NUTRITION FACTS

- Calories: 675 | Carbohydrates: 51.4g | Fat: 44.3g | Protein: 18.9g | Cholesterol: 158mg

INGREDIENTS

- 3 pounds chicken wings
- 1 egg, lightly beaten
- 1 cup all-purpose flour for coating
- 1 cup butter
- 3 tablespoons soy sauce

- 3 tablespoons water
- 1 cup white sugar
- 1/2 cup white vinegar
- 1/2 teaspoon garlic powder, or to taste
- 1 teaspoon salt

DIRECTIONS

1. Preheat oven to 350 degrees F (175 degrees C).
2. Cut wings in half, dip in egg and coat with flour.
3. Heat butter in a large, deep skillet over medium-high heat. Fry wings until deep brown. Place in a shallow roasting pan.
4. In a small bowl combine soy sauce, water, sugar, vinegar, garlic powder and salt. Pour over wings.
5. Bake in preheated oven for 30 to 45 minutes, basting wings with sauce often.

GRILLED BACON JALAPENO WRAPS

Servings: 6 | Prep: 10m | Cooks: 10m | Total: 20m

NUTRITION FACTS

Calories: 391 | Carbohydrates: 2.2g | Fat: 38.3g | Protein: 9.5g | Cholesterol: 79mg

INGREDIENTS

- 6 fresh jalapeno peppers, halved lengthwise and seeded
- 12 slices bacon

- 1 (8 ounce) package cream cheese

DIRECTIONS

1. Preheat an outdoor grill for high heat.
2. Spread cream cheese to fill jalapeno halves. Wrap with bacon. Secure with a toothpick.
3. Place on the grill, and cook until bacon is crispy.

CHOCOLATE CHIP CHEESE BALL
Servings: 32 | Prep: 20m | Cooks: 3h | Total: 3h20

NUTRITION FACTS

Calories: 102 | Carbohydrates: 6.9g | Fat: 8.4g | Protein: 1g | Cholesterol: 15mg

INGREDIENTS

- 1 (8 ounce) package cream cheese, softened
- 1/2 cup butter, softened
- 3/4 cup confectioners' sugar
- 2 tablespoons brown sugar
- 1/4 teaspoon vanilla extract
- 3/4 cup miniature semisweet chocolate chips
- 3/4 cup finely chopped pecans

DIRECTIONS

1. In a medium bowl, beat together cream cheese and butter until smooth. Mix in confectioners' sugar, brown sugar and vanilla. Stir in chocolate chips. Cover, and chill in the refrigerator for 2 hours.
2. Shape chilled cream cheese mixture into a ball. Wrap with plastic, and chill in the refrigerator for 1 hour.
3. Roll the cheese ball in finely chopped pecans before serving.

SPINACH BROWNIES
Servings: 24 | Prep: 20m | Cooks: 35m | Total: 55m

NUTRITION FACTS

Calories: 92 | Carbohydrates: 5.6g | Fat: 6g | Protein: 4.1g | Cholesterol: 32mg

INGREDIENTS

- 1 (10 ounce) package spinach, rinsed and chopped
- 1 cup all-purpose flour
- 1 teaspoon salt
- 1 teaspoon baking powder
- 2 eggs

- 1 cup milk
- 1/2 cup butter, melted
- 1 onion, chopped
- 1 (8 ounce) package shredded mozzarella cheese

DIRECTIONS

1. Preheat oven to 375 degrees F (190 degrees C). Lightly grease a 9x13 inch baking dish.
2. Place spinach in a medium saucepan with enough water to cover. Bring to a boil. Lower heat to simmer and cook until spinach is limp, about 3 minutes. Remove from heat, drain, and set aside.
3. In a large bowl, mix flour, salt and baking powder. Stir in eggs, milk and butter. Mix in spinach, onion and mozzarella cheese.
4. Transfer the mixture to the prepared baking dish. Bake in the preheated oven 30 to 35 minutes, or until a toothpick inserted in the center comes out clean. Cool before serving.

FLORENTINE ARTICHOKE DIP
Servings: 16 | Prep: 10m | Cooks: 25m | Total: 35m

NUTRITION FACTS

Calories: 194 | Carbohydrates: 4.9g | Fat: 17.1g | Protein: 6.1g | Cholesterol: 39mg

INGREDIENTS

- 1 (10 ounce) package frozen chopped spinach - thawed, drained and squeezed dry
- 1 (14 ounce) can artichoke hearts, drained and chopped
- 3 cloves garlic, minced
- 1/2 cup mayonnaise

- 2 (8 ounce) packages cream cheese, softened
- 2 tablespoons lemon juice
- 1 cup grated Parmesan cheese

DIRECTIONS

5. Preheat oven to 375 degrees F (190 degrees C). Lightly grease a 7x11 inch baking dish.

6. In a medium bowl, mix together the cream cheese and mayonnaise until smooth. Mix in the artichoke hearts, spinach and Parmesan cheese. Season with garlic and lemon juice. Spread evenly into the prepared baking dish.

7. Bake covered for 20 minutes. Remove the cover, and let the dish bake uncovered for 5 more minutes, or until the surface is lightly browned.

BEST EVER JALAPENO POPPERS

Servings: 32 | Prep: 45m | Cooks: 15m | Total: 1h

NUTRITION FACTS

Calories: 149 | Carbohydrates: 6.8g | Fat: 12g | Protein: 3.9g | Cholesterol: 20mg

INGREDIENTS

- 12 ounces cream cheese, softened
- 1 (8 ounce) package shredded Cheddar cheese
- 1 tablespoon bacon bits
- 12 ounces jalapeno peppers, seeded and halved
- 1 cup milk
- 1 cup all-purpose flour
- 1 cup dry bread crumbs
- 2 quarts oil for frying

DIRECTIONS

1. In a medium bowl, mix the cream cheese, Cheddar cheese and bacon bits. Spoon this mixture into the jalapeno pepper halves.
2. Put the milk and flour into two separate small bowls. Dip the stuffed jalapenos first into the milk then into the flour, making sure they are well coated with each. Allow the coated jalapenos to dry for about 10 minutes.
3. Dip the jalapenos in milk again and roll them through the breadcrumbs. Allow them to dry, then repeat to ensure the entire surface of the jalapeno is coated.
4. In a medium skillet, heat the oil to 365 degrees F (180 degrees C). Deep fry the coated jalapenos 2 to 3 minutes each, until golden brown. Remove and let drain on a paper towel.

AVOCADO, TOMATO AND MANGO SALSA

Servings: 6 | Prep: 15m | Cooks: 30m | Total: 45m

NUTRITION FACTS

Calories: 158 | Carbohydrates: 13.8g | Fat: 12g | Protein: 1.9g | Cholesterol: 0mg

INGREDIENTS

- 1 mango - peeled, seeded and diced
- 1 avocado - peeled, pitted, and diced
- 4 medium tomatoes, diced
- 3 cloves garlic, minced
- 1 teaspoon salt
- 2 tablespoons fresh lime juice

- 1 jalapeno pepper, seeded and minced
- 1/2 cup chopped fresh cilantro
- 1/4 cup chopped red onion
- 3 tablespoons olive oil

DIRECTIONS

1. In a medium bowl, combine the mango, avocado, tomatoes, jalapeno, cilantro, and garlic. Stir in the salt, lime juice, red onion, and olive oil. To blend the flavors, refrigerate for about 30 minutes before serving.

KEN'S PERFECT HARD BOILED EGG (AND I MEAN PERFECT)

Servings: 8 | Prep: 5m | Cooks: 20m | Total: 40m

NUTRITION FACTS

- Calories: 72 | Carbohydrates: 0.4g | Fat: 5g | Protein: 6.3g | Cholesterol: 186mg

INGREDIENTS

- 1 tablespoon salt
- 1/4 cup distilled white vinegar
- 6 cups water
- 8 eggs

DIRECTIONS

1. Combine the salt, vinegar, and water in a large pot, and bring to a boil over high heat. Add the eggs one at a time, being careful not to crack them. Reduce the heat to a gentle boil, and cook for 14 minutes.
2. Once the eggs have cooked, remove them from the hot water, and place into a container of ice water or cold, running water. Cool completely, about 15 minutes. Store in the refrigerator up to 1 week.

BACON AND TOMATO CUPS

Servings: 15 | Prep: 30m | Cooks: 12m | Total: 42m

NUTRITION FACTS

Calories: 216 | Carbohydrates: 15g | Fat: 15.1g | Protein: 5.3g | Cholesterol: 18mg

INGREDIENTS

- 8 slices bacon
- 1 tomato, chopped
- 1/2 onion, chopped
- 3 ounces shredded Swiss cheese
- 1/2 cup mayonnaise
- 1 teaspoon dried basil
- 1 (16 ounce) can refrigerated buttermilk biscuit dough

DIRECTIONS

1. Preheat oven to 375 degrees F (190 degrees C). Lightly grease a mini muffin pan.
2. In a skillet over medium heat, cook bacon until evenly brown. Drain on paper towels. Crumble bacon into a medium mixing bowl; add chopped tomato, onion, Swiss cheese, mayonnaise, and basil.
3. Separate biscuits into halves horizontally. Place each half into prepared mini muffin pan. Fill each biscuit half with the bacon mixture.
4. Bake in preheated oven until golden brown, 10 to 12 minutes.

TOASTED GARLIC BREAD
Servings: 10 | Prep: 10m | Cooks: 5m | Total: 15m

NUTRITION FACTS

Calories: 213 | Carbohydrates: 23.4g | Fat: 10.1g | Protein: 6.9g | Cholesterol: 22mg

INGREDIENTS

- 1 (1 pound) loaf Italian bread
- 5 tablespoons butter, softened
- 2 teaspoons extra virgin olive oil
- 3 cloves garlic, crushed
- 1 teaspoon dried oregano
- salt and pepper to taste
- 1 cup shredded mozzarella cheese

DIRECTIONS

1. Preheat the broiler.
2. Cut the bread into slices 1 to 2 inches thick.
3. In a small bowl, mix butter, olive oil, garlic, oregano, salt and pepper. Spread the mixture evenly on the bread slices.

4. On a medium baking sheet, arrange the slices evenly and broil 5 minutes, or until slightly brown. Check frequently so they do not burn.

5. Remove from broiler. Top with cheese and return to broiler 2 to 3 minutes, until cheese is slightly brown and melted. Serve at once.

SAUSAGE STUFFED JALAPENOS
Servings: 12 | Prep: 25m | Cooks: 20m | Total: 45m

NUTRITION FACTS

Calories: 362 | Carbohydrates: 4.3g | Fat: 34.3g | Protein: 9.2g | Cholesterol: 9.2mg

INGREDIENTS

- 1 pound ground pork sausage
- 1 (8 ounce) package cream cheese, softened
- 1 cup shredded Parmesan cheese
- 1 pound large fresh jalapeno peppers, halved lengthwise and seeded
- 1 (8 ounce) bottle Ranch dressing (optional)

DIRECTIONS

1. Preheat oven to 425 degrees F (220 degrees C).
2. Place sausage in a skillet over medium heat, and cook until evenly brown. Drain grease.
3. In a bowl, mix the sausage, cream cheese, and Parmesan cheese. Spoon about 1 tablespoon sausage mixture into each jalapeno half. Arrange stuffed halves in baking dishes.
4. Bake 20 minutes in the preheated oven, until bubbly and lightly browned. Serve with Ranch dressing.

PARTY PINWHEELS
Servings: 15 | Prep: 10m | Cooks: 5m | Total: 2h20m

NUTRITION FACTS

Calories: 229 | Carbohydrates: 18.6g | Fat: 14.5g | Protein: 5.9g | Cholesterol: 37mg

INGREDIENTS

- 2 (8 ounce) packages cream cheese, softened
- 1 (1 ounce) package ranch dressing mix
- 1/2 cup red bell pepper, diced
- 1/2 cup diced celery

- 2 green onions, minced
- 4 (12 inch) flour tortillas
- 1 (2 ounce) can sliced black olives
- 1/2 cup shredded Cheddar cheese

DIRECTIONS

1. In a medium-size mixing bowl, combine cream cheese, ranch dressing mix, and green onions. Spread this mixture on each tortilla. Sprinkle red pepper, celery, black olives, and cheese (if you'd like) over the cream cheese mixture. Roll up the tortillas, then wrap them tightly in aluminum foil.
2. Chill 2 hours or overnight. Cut off ends of the rolls, and slice the chilled rolls into 1 inch slices.

MY CRAB CAKES
Servings: 10 | Prep: 20m | Cooks: 10m | Total: 30m

NUTRITION FACTS

Calories: 318 | Carbohydrates: 22g | Fat: 22.1g | Protein: 10.5g | Cholesterol: 73mg

INGREDIENTS

- 2 tablespoons olive oil
- 6 green onions, chopped
- 3/8 cup olive oil
- 1 (16 ounce) can canned crabmeat, drained
- 1 egg
- 1 tablespoon mayonnaise
- ground black pepper to taste
- 1 teaspoon dry mustard
- 8 ounces buttery round crackers, crushed
- 1/2 teaspoon ground cayenne pepper
- 1 teaspoon garlic powder
- 1/4 teaspoon Old Bay Seasoning TM
- salt to taste
- 1 cup panko (Japanese bread crumbs) or regular dry bread crumbs

DIRECTIONS

1. Heat 2 tablespoons oil in a skillet over high heat. Saute green onions briefly until tender; cool slightly.
2. Combine crabmeat, sauteed green onions, egg, mayonnaise, dry mustard, crushed crackers, cayenne pepper, garlic powder, Old Bay seasoning, salt and pepper. Form into 1/2 inch thick patties. Coat the patties with bread crumbs.
3. Heat 1/2 cup oil in a skillet over medium high heat. Cook cakes until golden brown on each side. Drain briefly on paper towels and serve hot.

SPINACH QUICHE

S Servings: 6 | Prep: 20m | Cooks: 40m | Total: 1h

NUTRITION FACTS

Calories: 318 | Carbohydrates: 22g | Fat: 22.1g | Protein: 10.5g | Cholesterol: 73mg

INGREDIENTS

- 1/2 cup butter
- 3 cloves garlic, chopped
- 1 (4.5 ounce) can mushrooms, drained
- 1 (8 ounce) package shredded Cheddar cheese
- 1 (9 inch) unbaked deep dish pie crust
- 1 cup milk

- 1 small onion, chopped
- 1 (10 ounce) package frozen chopped spinach, thawed and drained
- 1 (6 ounce) package herb and garlic feta, crumbled
- salt and pepper to taste
- 4 eggs, beaten
- salt and pepper to taste

DIRECTIONS

1. Heat 2 tablespoons oil in a skillet over high heat. Saute green onions briefly until tender; cool slightly.
2. Combine crabmeat, sauteed green onions, egg, mayonnaise, dry mustard, crushed crackers, cayenne pepper, garlic powder, Old Bay seasoning, salt and pepper. Form into 1/2 inch thick patties. Coat the patties with bread crumbs.
3. Heat 1/2 cup oil in a skillet over medium high heat. Cook cakes until golden brown on each side. Drain briefly on paper towels and serve hot.

POTATO CHIPS

Servings: 4 | Prep: 30m | Cooks: 5m | Total: 35m

NUTRITION FACTS

Calories: 80 | Carbohydrates: 11.6g | Fat: 3.5g | Protein: 1.2g | Cholesterol: 0mg

INGREDIENTS

- 1 tablespoon vegetable oil
- 1 potato, sliced paper thin (peel optional)

- 1/2 teaspoon salt, or to taste

DIRECTIONS

1. Pour the vegetable oil into a plastic bag (a produce bag works well). Add the potato slices, and shake to coat.
2. Coat a large dinner plate lightly with oil or cooking spray. Arrange potato slices in a single layer on the dish.
3. Cook in the microwave for 3 to 5 minutes, or until lightly browned (if not browned, they will not become crisp). Times will vary depending on the power of your microwave. Remove chips from plate, and toss with salt (or other seasonings). Let cool. Repeat process with the remaining potato slices. You will not need to keep oiling the plate.

BONELESS BUFFALO WINGS
Servings: 3 | Prep: 10m | Cooks: 20m | Total: 50m | Additional: 20m

NUTRITION FACTS

Calories: 710 | Carbohydrates: 43.7g | Fat: 46.9g | Protein: 28g | Cholesterol: 136mg

INGREDIENTS

- oil for deep frying
- 1 cup unbleached all-purpose flour
- 2 teaspoons salt
- 1/2 teaspoon ground black pepper
- 1/2 teaspoon cayenne pepper
- 1/4 teaspoon garlic powder
- 1/2 teaspoon paprika
- 1 egg
- 1 cup milk
- 3 skinless, boneless chicken breasts, cut into 1/2-inch strips
- 1/4 cup hot pepper sauce
- 1 tablespoon butter

DIRECTIONS

1. Heat oil in a deep-fryer or large saucepan to 375 degrees F (190 degrees C).
2. Combine flour, salt, black pepper, cayenne pepper, garlic powder, and paprika in a large bowl. Whisk together the egg and milk in a small bowl. Dip each piece of chicken in the egg mixture, and then roll in the flour blend. Repeat so that each piece of chicken is double coated. Refrigerate breaded chicken for 20 minutes.
3. Fry chicken in the hot oil, in batches. Cook until the exterior is nicely browned, and the juices run clear, 5 to 6 minutes a batch.
4. Combine hot sauce and butter in a small bowl. Microwave sauce on High until melted, 20 to 30 seconds. Pour sauce over the cooked chicken; mix to coat.

SWEET AND SOUR MEATBALLS

Servings: 8 | Prep: 20m | Cooks: 35m | Total: 1h

NUTRITION FACTS

Calories: 427 | Carbohydrates: 42.1g | Fat: 16.5g | Protein: 27.4g | Cholesterol: 124g

INGREDIENTS

- 2 pounds lean ground beef
- 2 eggs
- 1 cup dry bread crumbs
- 1/2 cup finely chopped onion
- 1/2 teaspoon ground ginger
- 1 teaspoon seasoning salt
- 1/2 teaspoon ground black pepper
- 2 teaspoons Worcestershire sauce
- 1/2 teaspoon seasoning salt
- 1 large green bell pepper, cut into 1/2 inch pieces
- 2 teaspoons granulated sugar
- 1 (20 ounce) can pineapple chunks, drained with juice reserved
- 1/3 cup water
- 3 tablespoons distilled white vinegar
- 1 tablespoon soy sauce
- 1/2 cup packed brown sugar
- 3 tablespoons cornstarch
- 1/2 teaspoon ground ginger
- 1 large carrot, diced

DIRECTIONS

1. Preheat oven to 400 degrees F (200 degrees C). Lightly grease a large, shallow baking sheet.
2. In a large bowl, thoroughly mix the ground beef, eggs, bread crumbs and onion. Sprinkle with ginger, seasoning salt, pepper, Worcestershire sauce and sugar. Shape into one inch balls.
3. Place meatballs in a single layer on prepared baking sheet. Bake in preheated oven for 10 to 15 minutes; set aside.
4. To make the sauce, mix enough water with the reserved pineapple juice to make 1 cup. In a large pot over medium heat, combine the juice mixture, 1/3 cup water, vinegar, soy sauce, and brown sugar. Stir in cornstarch, ginger and seasoning salt, until smooth. Cover and cook until thickened.
5. Stir pineapple chunks, carrot, green pepper and meatballs into the sauce. Gently stir to coat the meatballs with the sauce. Simmer, uncovered, for about 20 minutes, or until meatballs are thoroughly cooked.

EASY GRANOLA BARS

Servings: 24 | Prep: 5m | Cooks: 20m | Total: 35m

NUTRITION FACTS

Calories: 179 | Carbohydrates: 24.8g | Fat: 8.1g | Protein: 3.9g | Cholesterol: 8mg

INGREDIENTS

- 3 cups quick-cooking oats
- 1 (14 ounce) can sweetened condensed milk
- 2 tablespoons butter, melted

- 1 cup flaked coconut

- 1 cup sliced almonds
- 1 cup miniature semisweet chocolate chips
- 1/2 cup sweetened dried cranberries

DIRECTIONS

1. Preheat oven to 350 degrees F (175 degrees C). Grease a 9x13 inch pan.
2. In a large bowl, mix together the oats, sweetened condensed milk, butter, coconut, almonds, chocolate chips and cranberries with your hands until well blended. Press flat into the prepared pan.
3. Bake for 20 to 25 minutes in the preheated oven, depending on how crunchy you want them. Lightly browned just around the edges will give you moist, chewy bars. Let cool for 5 minutes, cut into squares then let cool completely before serving.

GRILLED SHRIMP SCAMPI

Servings: 6 | Prep: 30m | Cooks: 6m | Total: 36m

NUTRITION FACTS

Calories: 173 | Carbohydrates: 1.6g | Fat: 10g | Protein: 18.7g | Cholesterol: 173mg

INGREDIENTS

- 1/4 cup olive oil
- 1/4 cup lemon juice
- 3 tablespoons chopped fresh parsley
- 1 tablespoon minced garlic

- ground black pepper to taste
- crushed red pepper flakes to taste (optional)
- 1 1/2 pounds medium shrimp, peeled and deveined

DIRECTIONS

1. In a large, non-reactive bowl, stir together the olive oil, lemon juice, parsley, garlic, and black pepper. Season with crushed red pepper, if desired. Add shrimp, and toss to coat. Marinate in the refrigerator for 30 minutes.
2. Preheat grill for high heat. Thread shrimp onto skewers, piercing once near the tail and once near the head. Discard any remaining marinade.
3. Lightly oil grill grate. Grill for 2 to 3 minutes per side, or until opaque.

CHICKEN WING DIP
Servings: 16 | Prep: 10m | Cooks: 30m | Total: 40m

NUTRITION FACTS

Calories: 240 | Carbohydrates: 1.6g | Fat: 21.8g | Protein: 9.4g | Cholesterol: 57mg

INGREDIENTS

- 2 (8 ounce) packages cream cheese, softened
- 3/4 cup pepper sauce (such as Frank's Red Hot®)
- 1 cup Ranch-style salad dressing

- 2 cups diced cooked chicken
- 1 cup shredded Cheddar cheese

DIRECTIONS

1. Preheat the oven to 350 degrees F (175 degrees C).
2. In a medium bowl, stir together the cream cheese and hot pepper sauce until well blended. Mix in the Ranch dressing, chicken and Cheddar cheese. Spread into a 9x13 inch baking dish.
3. Bake for 30 minutes in the preheated oven. If oil collects on the top, dab it off using a paper towel. Serve with tortilla chips.

HOT PIZZA DIP
Servings: 16 | Prep: 10m | Cooks: 5m | Total: 15m

NUTRITION FACTS

Calories: 115 | Carbohydrates: 1.9g | Fat: 9.5g | Protein: 5.6g | Cholesterol: 29mg

INGREDIENTS

- 1 (8 ounce) package cream cheese, softened
- 1/2 teaspoon dried oregano

- 1 cup grated Parmesan cheese
- 1 cup pizza sauce

- 1/2 teaspoon dried parsley
- 1/4 teaspoon dried basil
- 1 cup shredded mozzarella cheese
- 2 tablespoons chopped green bell pepper
- 2 ounces pepperoni sausage, chopped
- 2 tablespoons sliced black olives

DIRECTIONS

1. In a small bowl, mix together the cream cheese, oregano, parsley, and basil.
2. Spread mixture in the bottom of a 9 inch pie plate, or a shallow microwave-safe dish. Sprinkle 1/2 cup of the mozzarella cheese and 1/2 cup of the Parmesan cheese on top of the cream cheese mixture. Spread the pizza sauce over all. Sprinkle with remaining cheese, then top with green pepper, pepperoni and olive slices. Cover, and microwave for 5 minutes. Serve hot.

BAKED HAM AND CHEESE PARTY SANDWICHES
Servings: 24 | Prep: 15m | Cooks: 20m | Total: 35m

NUTRITION FACTS

Calories: 208 | Carbohydrates: 10.8g | Fat: 14g | Protein: 9.8g | Cholesterol: 43mg

INGREDIENTS

- 3/4 cup melted butter
- 1 1/2 tablespoons Dijon mustard
- 1 1/2 teaspoons Worcestershire sauce
- 1 1/2 tablespoons poppy seeds
- 1 tablespoon dried minced onion
- 24 mini sandwich rolls
- 1 pound thinly sliced cooked deli ham
- 1 pound thinly sliced Swiss cheese

DIRECTIONS

1. Preheat oven to 350 degrees F (175 degrees C). Grease a 9x13-inch baking dish.
2. In a bowl, mix together butter, Dijon mustard, Worcestershire sauce, poppy seeds, and dried onion. Separate the tops from bottoms of the rolls, and place the bottom pieces into the prepared baking dish. Layer about half the ham onto the rolls. Arrange the Swiss cheese over the ham, and top with remaining ham slices in a layer. Place the tops of the rolls onto the sandwiches. Pour the mustard mixture evenly over the rolls.
3. Bake in the preheated oven until the rolls are lightly browned and the cheese has melted, about 20 minutes. Slice into individual rolls through the ham and cheese layers to serve.

LUSCIOUS SPINACH ARTICHOKE DIP

Servings: 24 | Prep: 10m | Cooks: 25m | Total: 35m

NUTRITION FACTS

Calories: 50 | Carbohydrates: 2.4g | Fat: 4g | Protein: 1.5g | Cholesterol: 7mg

INGREDIENTS

- 1 (14 ounce) can artichoke hearts, drained and chopped
- 1/2 (10 ounce) package frozen chopped spinach, thawed
- 1/2 cup sour cream
- 1/4 cup mayonnaise
- 1/4 cup cream cheese
- 1/4 cup grated Romano cheese
- 1/4 teaspoon minced garlic

DIRECTIONS

1. Preheat oven to 375 degrees F (190 degrees C).
2. In a small baking dish, mix together artichoke hearts, spinach, sour cream, mayonnaise, cream cheese, Romano cheese, and garlic. Cover dish.
3. Bake until heated through and bubbly, about 25 minutes.

BAKED CHICKEN WINGS

Servings: 2 | Prep: 10m | Cooks: 1h | Total: 1h10m | Servings: 2

NUTRITION FACTS

Calories: 532 | Carbohydrates: 3.9g | Fat: 43.1g | Protein: 31.7g | Cholesterol: 97mg

INGREDIENTS

- 3 tablespoons olive oil
- 3 cloves garlic, pressed
- 2 teaspoons chili powder
- 1 teaspoon garlic powder
- salt and ground black pepper to taste
- 10 chicken wings

DIRECTIONS

1. Preheat the oven to 375 degrees F (190 degrees C).

2. Combine the olive oil, garlic, chili powder, garlic powder, salt, and pepper in a large, resealable bag; seal and shake to combine. Add the chicken wings; reseal and shake to coat. Arrange the chicken wings on a baking sheet.

3. Cook the wings in the preheated oven 1 hour, or until crisp and cooked through.

AVOCADO FETA SALSA

Servings: 12 | Prep: 20m | Cooks: 2h | Total: 2h20m

NUTRITION FACTS

Calories: 66 | Carbohydrates: 2.8g | Fat: 5.6g | Protein: 1.8g | Cholesterol: 8mg

INGREDIENTS

- 2 plum tomatoes, chopped
- 1 ripe avocado - peeled, pitted and chopped
- 1/4 cup finely chopped red onion
- 1 clove garlic, minced
- 1 tablespoon snipped fresh parsley
- 1 tablespoon chopped fresh oregano
- 1 tablespoon olive oil
- 1 tablespoon red or white wine vinegar
- 4 ounces crumbled feta cheese

DIRECTIONS

1. In a bowl, gently stir together tomatoes, avocados, onion, and garlic. Mix in parsley and oregano. Gently stir in olive oil and vinegar. Then stir in feta. Cover, and chill for 2 to 6 hours.

QUICK BAKED ZUCCHINI CHIPS

Servings: 4 | Prep: 5m | Cooks: 10m | Total: 15m

NUTRITION FACTS

Calories: 92 | Carbohydrates: 13.8g | Fat: 1.7g | Protein: 6.1g | Cholesterol: 2mg

INGREDIENTS

- 2 medium zucchini, cut into 1/4-inch slices
- 1/2 cup seasoned dry bread crumbs
- 1/8 teaspoon ground black pepper
- 2 tablespoons grated Parmesan cheese
- 2 egg whites

DIRECTIONS

1. Preheat the oven to 475 degrees F (245 degrees C).
2. In one small bowl, stir together the bread crumbs, pepper and Parmesan cheese. Place the egg whites in a separate bowl. Dip zucchini slices into the egg whites, then coat the breadcrumb mixture. Place on a greased baking sheet.
3. Bake for 5 minutes in the preheated oven, then turn over and bake for another 5 to 10 minutes, until browned and crispy.

FRIED MOZZARELLA CHEESE STICKS
Servings: 8 | Prep: 15m | Cooks: 15m | Total: 30m

NUTRITION FACTS

Calories: 400 | Carbohydrates: 29.5g | Fat: 22.5g | Protein: 19.4g | Cholesterol: 83mg

INGREDIENTS

- 2 eggs, beaten
- 1/4 cup water
- 1 1/2 cups Italian seasoned bread crumbs
- 1/2 teaspoon garlic salt

- 1/3 cup cornstarch
- 1 quart oil for deep frying
- 1 (16 ounce) package mozzarella cheese sticks
- 2/3 cup all-purpose flour

DIRECTIONS

1. In a small bowl, mix the eggs and water.
2. Mix the bread crumbs and garlic salt in a medium bowl. In a medium bowl, blend the flour and cornstarch.
3. In a large heavy saucepan, heat the oil to 365 degrees F (185 degrees C).
4. One at a time, coat each mozzarella stick in the flour mixture, then the egg mixture, then in the bread crumbs and finally into the oil. Fry until golden brown, about 30 seconds. Remove from heat and drain on paper towels.

ANTIPASTO SQUARES
Servings: 10 | Prep: 15m | Cooks: 45m | Total: 1h

NUTRITION FACTS

Calories: 452 | Carbohydrates: 25.3g | Fat: 29.1g | Protein: 20g | Cholesterol: 104mg

INGREDIENTS

- 2 (10 ounce) cans refrigerated crescent dinner rolls
- 1/4 pound thinly sliced boiled ham
- 1/4 pound thinly sliced pepperoni sausage
- 3 eggs
- 1/2 teaspoon ground black pepper

- 1/4 pound thinly sliced Swiss cheese
- 1/4 pound thinly sliced Genoa salami
- 1 (12 ounce) jar roasted red peppers, drained, cut into thin strips
- 3 tablespoons grated Parmesan cheese
- 1/4 pound thinly sliced provolone cheese

DIRECTIONS

1. Preheat oven to 350 degrees F (175 C).
2. Unroll one package of crescent roll dough, and cover the bottom of a 9x13 inch pan. Layer the ham, provolone cheese, Swiss cheese, salami, pepperoni, and red peppers, on top of the dough.
3. In a bowl, beat the eggs lightly, and stir in the parmesan cheese and black pepper. Pour 3/4 of this mixture over the peppers. Unroll the second package of dough, and place over the top of the peppers. Brush with the remaining egg mixture. Cover with aluminum foil.
4. Bake for 25 minutes in the preheated oven. Remove foil, and bake another 10 to 20 minutes, or until dough is fluffy and golden brown. Cut into squares. Serve warm, or at room temperature.

THE BEST SWEET AND SOUR MEATBALLS
Servings: 4 | Prep: 20m | Cooks: 30m | Total: 1h

NUTRITION FACTS

Calories: 516 | Carbohydrates: 67.1g | Fat: 16.8g | Protein: 24.5g | Cholesterol: 122mg

INGREDIENTS

- 1 pound ground beef
- 1 egg
- 1/4 cup dry bread crumbs
- 1 onion, diced
- 3 tablespoons soy sauce

- 1 cup packed brown sugar
- 3 tablespoons all-purpose flour
- 1 1/2 cups water
- 1/4 cup distilled white vinegar

DIRECTIONS

1. In a medium bowl, combine the ground beef, egg, bread crumbs and onion. Mix thoroughly and shape into golf ball-sized balls.
2. In a large skillet over medium heat, gently brown the meatballs and set aside.
3. In a large saucepan, combine the brown sugar, flour, water, white vinegar and soy sauce. Mix thoroughly. Add meatballs and bring to a boil. Reduce heat and simmer, stirring often, for 30 minutes.

FRESH TOMATO SALSA
Servings: 4 | Prep: 10m | Cooks: 1h | Total: 1h10m

NUTRITION FACTS

Calories: 51 | Carbohydrates: 9.7g | Fat: 0.2g | Protein: 2.1g | Cholesterol: 0mg

INGREDIENTS

- 3 tomatoes, chopped
- 1/2 cup finely diced onion
- 5 serrano chiles, finely chopped
- 1/2 cup chopped fresh cilantro
- 1 teaspoon salt
- 2 teaspoons lime juice

DIRECTIONS

1. In a medium bowl, stir together tomatoes, onion, chili peppers, cilantro, salt, and lime juice. Chill for one hour in the refrigerator before serving.

MAHOGANY CHICKEN WINGS
Servings: 5 | Prep: 15m | Cooks: 50m | Total: 1h5m

NUTRITION FACTS

Calories: 773 | Carbohydrates: 43.1g | Fat: 43.6g | Protein: 51.9g | Cholesterol: 210mg

INGREDIENTS

- 3 pounds chicken wings, split and tips discarded
- 1/2 cup soy sauce
- 1/2 cup honey
- 1/4 cup molasses
- 2 tablespoons chile sauce
- 1 teaspoon ground ginger
- 2 cloves garlic, finely chopped

DIRECTIONS

1. Place chicken in a shallow, medium dish.
2. In a medium bowl, mix soy sauce, honey, molasses, chile sauce, ground ginger and garlic. Pour the mixture over the chicken. Cover and refrigerate approximately 1 hour, turning occasionally.
3. Preheat oven to 375 degrees F (190 degrees C).
4. In a large baking dish, arrange chicken in a single layer. Bake in the preheated oven approximately 50 minutes, brushing with remaining soy sauce mixture often and turning once, until meat is no longer pink and juices run clear.

VIETNAMESE FRESH SPRING ROLLS
Servings: 8 | Prep: 45m | Cooks: 5m | Total: 50m

NUTRITION FACTS

Calories: 82 | Carbohydrates: 15.8g | Fat: 0.7g | Protein: 3.3g | Cholesterol: 0mg

INGREDIENTS

- 2 ounces rice vermicelli
- 8 rice wrappers (8.5 inch diameter)
- 8 large cooked shrimp - peeled, deveined and cut in half
- 1 1/3 tablespoons chopped fresh Thai basil
- 3 tablespoons chopped fresh mint leaves
- 1 clove garlic, minced
- 1/2 teaspoon garlic chili sauce
- 1 teaspoon finely chopped peanuts

- 3 tablespoons chopped fresh cilantro
- 2 leaves lettuce, chopped
- 4 teaspoons fish sauce
- 1/4 cup water
- 2 tablespoons fresh lime juice
- 2 tablespoons white sugar
- 3 tablespoons hoisin sauce

DIRECTIONS

1. Bring a medium saucepan of water to boil. Boil rice vermicelli 3 to 5 minutes, or until al dente, and drain.
2. Fill a large bowl with warm water. Dip one wrapper into the hot water for 1 second to soften. Lay wrapper flat. In a row across the center, place 2 shrimp halves, a handful of vermicelli, basil, mint, cilantro and lettuce, leaving about 2 inches uncovered on each side. Fold uncovered sides inward, then tightly roll the wrapper, beginning at the end with the lettuce. Repeat with remaining ingredients.
3. In a small bowl, mix the fish sauce, water, lime juice, garlic, sugar and chili sauce.
4. In another small bowl, mix the hoisin sauce and peanuts.
5. Serve rolled spring rolls with the fish sauce and hoisin sauce mixtures.

HOT ARTICHOKE SPINACH DIP
Servings: 16 | Prep: 20m | Cooks: 25m | Total: 45m

NUTRITION FACTS

Calories: 82 | Carbohydrates: 3.1g | Fat: 6g | Protein: 4.3g | Cholesterol: 19mg

INGREDIENTS

- 1 (14 ounce) can artichoke hearts, drained
- 1/3 cup grated Romano cheese
- 1/4 cup grated Parmesan cheese
- 1/2 teaspoon minced garlic
- 1/3 cup heavy cream
- 1/2 cup sour cream
- 1 cup shredded mozzarella cheese
- 1 (10 ounce) package frozen chopped spinach, thawed and drained

DIRECTIONS

1. Preheat oven to 350 degrees F (175 degrees C). Grease a 9x13 inch baking dish.
2. In a blender or food processor, place artichoke hearts, Romano cheese, Parmesan cheese and garlic . Pulse until chopped, but not ground. Set aside.
3. In a medium bowl, mix together spinach, heavy cream, sour cream and mozzarella cheese. Stir in artichoke mixture. Spoon into prepared baking dish.
4. Bake in the preheated oven for 20 to 25 minutes, or until cheese is melted and bubbly.

BEST GUACAMOLE
Servings: 16 | Prep: 5m | Cooks: 1h | Total: 1h5m

NUTRITION FACTS

Calories: 56 | Carbohydrates: 2.6g | Fat: 5.4g | Protein: 0.6g | Cholesterol: 0mg

INGREDIENTS

- 2 avocados
- 1/2 lemon, juiced
- 2 tablespoons chopped onion
- 1/2 teaspoon salt
- 2 tablespoons olive oil

DIRECTIONS

1. Cut the avocados into halves. Remove the seeds, and scoop out the pulp into a small bowl. Use a fork to mash the avocado. Stir in lemon juice, onion, salt, and olive oil. Cover the bowl, and refrigerate for 1 hour before serving.

HOT BEAN DIP

Servings: 20 | Prep: 10m | Cooks: 30m | Total: 40m

NUTRITION FACTS

Calories: 196 | Carbohydrates: 8.6g | Fat: 14g | Protein: 9.3g | Cholesterol: 43mg

INGREDIENTS

- 1 (8 ounce) package cream cheese, softened
- 1 cup sour cream
- 2 (16 ounce) cans refried beans
- 1/2 (1 ounce) package taco seasoning mix
- 5 drops hot pepper sauce
- 2 tablespoons dried parsley
- 1/4 cup chopped green onions
- 1 (8 ounce) package shredded Cheddar cheese
- 1 (8 ounce) package shredded Monterey Jack cheese

DIRECTIONS

1. Preheat oven to 350 degrees F (175 degrees C).
2. In a medium bowl, blend the cream cheese and sour cream. Mix in the refried beans, taco seasoning, hot pepper sauce, parsley, green onions, 1/2 the Cheddar cheese and 1/2 the Monterey Jack cheese. Transfer the mixture to an 8x12 inch baking dish. Top with remaining Cheddar and Monterey Jack cheeses.
3. Bake in the preheated oven 20 to 30 minutes, until cheese is slightly browned.

CANDIED PECANS

Servings: 10 | Prep: 10m | Cooks: 1h | Total: 1h10m

NUTRITION FACTS

Calories: 393 | Carbohydrates: 26.5g | Fat: 32.7g | Protein: 4.5g | Cholesterol: 0mg

INGREDIENTS

- 1 cup white sugar
- 1 teaspoon ground cinnamon
- 1 teaspoon salt
- 1 egg white
- 1 tablespoon water
- 1 pound pecan halves

DIRECTIONS

1. Preheat oven to 250 degrees F (120 degrees C).
2. Mix sugar, cinnamon, and salt together in a bowl.
3. Whisk egg white and water together in a separate bowl until frothy. Toss pecans in the egg white mixture. Mix sugar mixture into pecan mixture until pecans are evenly coated. Spread coated pecans onto a baking sheet.
4. Bake in the preheated oven, stirring every 15 minutes, until pecans are evenly browned, 1 hour.

CRAB DIP
Servings: 16 | Prep: 15m | Cooks: 30m | Total: 45m

NUTRITION FACTS

Calories: 198 | Carbohydrates: 15.3g | Fat: 11.5g | Protein: 8.4g | Cholesterol: 42mg

INGREDIENTS

- 11 ounces cream cheese, softened
- 1 small onion, finely chopped
- 5 tablespoons mayonnaise
- 2 (6 ounce) cans crabmeat, drained and flaked
- 1/8 teaspoon garlic powder
- salt and pepper to taste
- 1 (1 pound) loaf round, crusty Italian bread

DIRECTIONS

1. Preheat oven to 350 degrees F (175 degrees C).
2. In a medium bowl, combine the cream cheese, onion, mayonnaise, crabmeat, garlic powder, salt and pepper. Spread mixture into a 1 quart baking dish.
3. Bake for 20 minutes in the preheated oven. While the dip is baking, cut a circle in the top of the bread, and scoop out the inside to create a bread bowl. Tear the removed bread into pieces for dipping.
4. Remove baked crab dip from the oven, and stir well. Spoon the mixture into the hollowed out loaf. Place bread bowl and chunks of bread on a medium baking sheet, and bake for an additional 10 minutes. Serve hot.

NACHO CHEESE SAUCE
Servings: 4 | Prep: 10m | Cooks: 15m | Total: 25m

NUTRITION FACTS

Calories: 282 | Carbohydrates: 6.6g | Fat: 22.5g | Protein: 13.5g | Cholesterol: 67mg

INGREDIENTS

- 2 tablespoons butter
- 2 tablespoons all-purpose flour
- 1 cup milk
- 7 slices processed American cheese
- 1/2 teaspoon salt

DIRECTIONS

1. In a medium saucepan over medium heat, melt butter and stir in flour. Pour in the milk and stir until the mixture thickens. Stirring constantly, mix in cheese and salt. Continue to cook and stir until cheese has melted and all ingredients are well blended, about 15 minutes.

DAWN'S CANDIED WALNUTS

Servings: 16 | Prep: 10m | Cooks: 20m | Total: 30m

NUTRITION FACTS

Calories: 238 | Carbohydrates: 16.9g | Fat: 18.6g | Protein: 4.5g | Cholesterol: < 1mg

INGREDIENTS

- 1 pound walnut halves
- 1 cup white sugar
- 2 teaspoons ground cinnamon
- 1/4 teaspoon salt
- 6 tablespoons milk
- 1 teaspoon vanilla extract

DIRECTIONS

1. Preheat oven to 350 degrees F (175 degrees C). Spread nuts in a single layer over a baking sheet. Roast for approximately 8 to 10 minutes, or until the nuts start to turn brown and the smell of roasting nuts fills the kitchen.
2. Stir together sugar, cinnamon, salt, and milk in a medium saucepan. Cook over medium-high heat for 8 minutes, or until the mixture reaches the soft ball stage of 236 degrees F (113 degrees C). Remove from heat, and stir in vanilla immediately. .
3. Add walnuts to sugar syrup, and stir to coat well. Spoon nuts onto waxed paper, and immediately separate nuts with a fork. Cool, and store in airtight containers.

VICKI'S HUSH PUPPIES

Servings: 8 | Prep: 10m | Cooks: 30m | Total: 40m

NUTRITION FACTS

Calories: 277 | Carbohydrates: 36.7g | Fat: 12.9g | Protein: 4.6g | Cholesterol: 46mg

INGREDIENTS

- 2 eggs, beaten
- 1/2 cup white sugar
- 1 large onion, diced
- 1 cup self-rising cornmeal
- 1 quart oil for frying
- 1 cup self-rising flour

DIRECTIONS

1. In a medium bowl, mix together eggs, sugar, and onion. Blend in flour and cornmeal.
2. Heat 2 inches of oil to 365 degrees F (185 degrees C). Drop batter by rounded teaspoonfuls in hot oil, and fry until golden brown. Cook in small batches to maintain oil temperature. Drain briefly on paper towels. Serve hot.

GARY'S STUFFED MUSHROOMS

Servings: 12 | Prep: 30m | Cooks: 12m | Total: 42m

NUTRITION FACTS

Calories: 413 | Carbohydrates: 14.4g | Fat: 37.9g | Protein: 5.9g | Cholesterol: 106mg

INGREDIENTS

- 12 large fresh mushrooms, stems removed
- 1 (6 ounce) package chicken flavored dry stuffing mix
- 1 (8 ounce) package cream cheese, softened
- 1/2 pound imitation crabmeat, flaked
- 2 cups butter
- 2 cloves garlic, peeled and minced
- salt and pepper to taste
- garlic powder to taste
- crushed red pepper to taste

DIRECTIONS

1. Arrange mushroom caps on a medium baking sheet, bottoms up. Chop and reserve mushroom stems.
2. Prepare chicken flavored dry stuffing mix according to package directions.
3. Preheat oven to 350 degrees F (175 degrees C).
4. In a medium saucepan over medium heat, melt butter. Mix in garlic and cook until tender, about 5 minutes.
5. In a medium bowl, mix together reserved mushroom stems, prepared dry stuffing mix, cream cheese and imitation crabmeat. Liberally stuff mushrooms with the mixture. Drizzle with the butter and garlic. Season with salt, pepper, garlic powder and crushed red pepper.
6. Bake uncovered in the preheated oven 10 to 12 minutes, or until stuffing is lightly browned.

BEST BRUSCHETTA EVER
Servings: 8 | Prep: 20m | Cooks: 8h | Total: 8h20m

NUTRITION FACTS

Calories: 47 | Carbohydrates: 1.5g | Fat: 4.2g | Protein: 1.3g | Cholesterol: 2mg

INGREDIENTS

- 2 tomatoes, cubed
- 1 teaspoon dried basil
- 4 tablespoons grated Parmesan cheese
- 2 tablespoons olive oil

- 1 clove garlic, crushed
- seasoning salt to taste
- ground black pepper to taste

DIRECTIONS

1. In a medium bowl, mix tomatoes, dried basil, Parmesan cheese, olive oil, garlic, seasoning salt and ground black pepper. Cover and chill in the refrigerator 8 hours, or overnight, before serving.

DI'S DELICIOUS DELUXE DEVILED EGGS
Servings: 12 | Prep: 20m | Cooks: 15m | Total: 45m

NUTRITION FACTS

Calories: 70 | Carbohydrates: 0.6g | Fat: 6.1g | Protein: 3.2g | Cholesterol: 23mg

INGREDIENTS

- 6 eggs

- 1/4 cup mayonnaise

- 1/2 stalk celery, finely chopped
- 1 dash hot pepper sauce
- 1/4 onion, finely chopped
- salt to taste
- paprika, for garnish

DIRECTIONS

1. Place eggs in a medium saucepan and cover with cold water. Bring water to a boil and immediately remove from heat. Cover and let eggs stand in hot water for 10 to 12 minutes. Remove from hot water, cool and peel.
2. Cut eggs in half. Remove yolks and place in a medium bowl. Mash together with celery, onion, mayonnaise, salt and hot pepper sauce.
3. Stuff the egg white halves with the egg yolk mixture. Sprinkle eggs with paprika. Chill covered in the refrigerator until serving.

TOMATILLO SALSA VERDE
Servings: 8 | Prep: 10m | Cooks: 15m | Total: 25m

NUTRITION FACTS

Calories: 24 | Carbohydrates: 4.6g | Fat: 0.6g | Protein: 0.8g | Cholesterol: 0mg

INGREDIENTS

- 1 pound tomatillos, husked
- 1/2 cup finely chopped onion
- 1 teaspoon minced garlic
- 1 serrano chile peppers, minced
- 2 tablespoons chopped cilantro
- 1 1/2 teaspoons salt, or to taste
- 2 cups water
- 1 tablespoon chopped fresh oregano
- 1/2 teaspoon ground cumin

DIRECTIONS

1. Place tomatillos, onion, garlic, and chile pepper into a saucepan. Season with cilantro, oregano, cumin, and salt; pour in water. Bring to a boil over high heat, then reduce heat to medium-low, and simmer until the tomatillos are soft, 10 to 15 minutes.
2. Using a blender, carefully puree the tomatillos and water in batches until smooth.

CHICKEN ENCHILADA DIP

Servings: 30 | Prep: 15m | Cooks: 50m | Total: 1h15m | Additional: 10m

NUTRITION FACTS

Calories: 128 | Carbohydrates: 0.8g | Fat: 11.5g | Protein: 5.7g | Cholesterol: 28mg

INGREDIENTS

- 1 pound skinless, boneless chicken breast halves
- 1 (8 ounce) package cream cheese, softened
- 1 (8 ounce) jar mayonnaise
- 1 (8 ounce) package shredded Cheddar cheese
- 1 (4 ounce) can diced green chile peppers
- 1 jalapeno pepper, finely diced

DIRECTIONS

1. Preheat oven to 350 degrees F (175 degrees C). Place chicken breast halves on a medium baking sheet.

2. Bake in the preheated oven 20 minutes, or until no longer pink. Remove from heat, cool and shred.

3. Place shredded chicken in a medium bowl, and mix in cream cheese, mayonnaise, Cheddar cheese, green chile peppers and jalapeno pepper. Transfer the chicken mixture to a medium baking dish.

4. Bake uncovered in the preheated oven 30 minutes, or until the edges are golden brown.

ROASTED GARLIC BREAD

Servings: 8 | Prep: 15m | Cooks: 35m | Total: 50m

NUTRITION FACTS

Calories: 322 | Carbohydrates: 35.4g | Fat: 17.3g | Protein: 6.9g | Cholesterol: 32mg

INGREDIENTS

- 3 heads garlic
- 2 tablespoons olive oil
- 1 (1 pound) loaf Italian bread
- 1/2 cup butter
- 1 tablespoon chopped fresh parsley (optional)
- 2 tablespoons grated Parmesan cheese (optional)

DIRECTIONS

1. Preheat the oven to 350 degrees F (175 degrees C). Slice the tops off of garlic heads so the tip of each clove is exposed. Place garlic on a baking sheet and drizzle with olive oil. Bake until garlic is soft, about 30 minutes.
2. Set the oven to broil. Slice the loaf of bread in half horizontally, and place cut-side up on a baking sheet.
3. Squeeze the cloves of garlic from their skins into a medium bowl. Stir in the butter, parsley, and Parmesan cheese until well blended. Spread onto the cut sides of the bread.
4. Broil bread until toasted, about 5 minutes.

PITA CHIPS
Servings: 24 | Prep: 10m | Cooks: 7m | Total: 17m

NUTRITION FACTS

Calories: 125 | Carbohydrates: 17.7g | Fat: 5.3g | Protein: 3.2g | Cholesterol: 0mg

INGREDIENTS

- 12 pita bread pockets
- 1/2 cup olive oil
- 1/2 teaspoon ground black pepper

- 1 teaspoon garlic salt
- 1/2 teaspoon dried basil
- 1 teaspoon dried chervil

DIRECTIONS

1. Preheat oven to 400 degrees F (200 degrees C).
2. Cut each pita bread into 8 triangles. Place triangles on lined cookie sheet.
3. In a small bowl, combine the oil, pepper, salt, basil and chervil. Brush each triangle with oil mixture.
4. Bake in the preheated oven for about 7 minutes, or until lightly browned and crispy. Watch carefully, as they tend to burn easily!

PICO DE GALLO
Servings: 12 | Prep: 20m | Cooks: 3h | Total: 3h20m

NUTRITION FACTS

Calories: 10 | Carbohydrates: 2.2g | Fat: 0.1g | Protein: 0.4g | Cholesterol: 0mg

INGREDIENTS

- 6 roma (plum) tomatoes, diced
- 1 clove garlic, minced

- 1/2 red onion, minced
- 3 tablespoons chopped fresh cilantro
- 1/2 jalapeno pepper, seeded and minced
- 1/2 lime, juiced
- 1 pinch garlic powder
- 1 pinch ground cumin, or to taste
- salt and ground black pepper to taste

DIRECTIONS

1. Stir the tomatoes, onion, cilantro, jalapeno pepper, lime juice, garlic, garlic powder, cumin, salt, and pepper together in a bowl. Refrigerate at least 3 hours before serving.

HOT MEXICAN SPINACH DIP
Servings: 58 | Prep: 15m | Cooks: 15m | Total: 30m

NUTRITION FACTS

Calories: 40 | Carbohydrates: 1.4g | Fat: 3.1g | Protein: 1.9g | Cholesterol: 9mg

INGREDIENTS

- 1 (16 ounce) jar salsa
- 1 (10 ounce) package frozen chopped spinach, thawed and drained
- 2 cups shredded Monterey Jack cheese
- 1 (8 ounce) package cream cheese, diced and softened
- 1 cup evaporated milk
- 1 (2.25 ounce) can chopped black olives, drained
- 1 tablespoon red wine vinegar
- salt and pepper to taste

DIRECTIONS

1. Preheat oven to 400 degrees F (200 degrees C).
2. In a medium baking dish, mix together salsa, chopped spinach, Monterey Jack cheese, cream cheese, evaporated milk, black olives, red wine vinegar, salt and pepper.
3. Bake mixture in the preheated oven 12 to 15 minutes, or until bubbly.

SLOW COOKER REUBEN DIP
Servings: 12 | Prep: 4m | Cooks: 45m | Total: 49m

NUTRITION FACTS

Calories: 298 | Carbohydrates: 5.5g | Fat: 22.9g | Protein: 17.9g | Cholesterol: 76mg

INGREDIENTS

- 1 (16 ounce) jar sauerkraut, drained
- 1 (8 ounce) package cream cheese, softened
- 2 cups shredded Swiss cheese
- 2 cups shredded cooked corned beef
- 1/4 cup thousand island dressing

DIRECTIONS

1. In a slow cooker, combine the sauerkraut, cream cheese, Swiss cheese, corned beef and thousand island dressing. Cover, and cook on high for 45 minutes if you're in a hurry, low for longer if you're not, or just until hot and cheese is melted. Stir occasionally while cooking. Serve with cocktail rye or crackers.

ROASTED CHICKPEAS
Servings: 4 | Prep: 5m | Cooks: 40h | Total: 45m

NUTRITION FACTS

Calories: 161 | Carbohydrates: 19.3g | Fat: 7.7g | Protein: 4.2g | Cholesterol: 0mg

INGREDIENTS

- 1 (12 ounce) can chickpeas (garbanzo beans), drained
- 2 tablespoons olive oil
- salt (optional)
- garlic salt (optional)
- cayenne pepper (optional)

DIRECTIONS

1. Preheat oven to 450 degrees F (230 degrees C).
2. Blot chickpeas with a paper towel to dry them. In a bowl, toss chickpeas with olive oil, and season to taste with salt, garlic salt, and cayenne pepper, if using. Spread on a baking sheet, and bake for 30 to 40 minutes, until browned and crunchy. Watch carefully the last few minutes to avoid burning.

SPECIAL DEVILED EGGS
Servings: 6 | Prep: 10m | Cooks: 12m | Total: 22m

Calories: 151 | Carbohydrates: 4g | Fat: 12.4g | Protein: 6.6g | Cholesterol: 189mg

INGREDIENTS

- 6 eggs
- 1/4 cup mayonnaise
- 2 tablespoons finely chopped onion
- 3 tablespoons sweet pickle relish
- 1 tablespoon prepared horseradish
- 1 tablespoon prepared mustard
- paprika, for garnish
- salt and pepper to taste

DIRECTIONS

1. Place eggs in a medium saucepan and cover with cold water. Bring water to a boil and immediately remove from heat. Cover and let eggs stand in hot water for 10 to 12 minutes. Remove from hot water, cool, peel and cut lengthwise.
2. Remove yolks from eggs. In a medium bowl, mash the yolks and mix together with mayonnaise, onion, sweet pickle relish, horseradish and mustard.
3. With a fork or pastry bag, fill the egg halves with the yolk mixture. Garnish with paprika, salt and pepper. Chill until serving.

GREAT GARLIC BREAD

Servings: 8 | Prep: 10m | Cooks: 15m | Total: 25m

NUTRITION FACTS

Calories: 332 | Carbohydrates: 30.4g | Fat: 18g | Protein: 12.2g | Cholesterol: 48mg

INGREDIENTS

- 1/2 cup butter
- 1 1/2 tablespoons garlic powder
- 1 tablespoon dried parsley
- 1 (1 pound) loaf Italian bread, cut into 1/2 inch slices
- 1 (8 ounce) package shredded mozzarella cheese

DIRECTIONS

1. Preheat oven to 350 degrees F (175 degrees C).

2. In a small saucepan over medium heat, melt butter and mix with garlic powder and dried parsley.

3. Place Italian bread on a medium baking sheet. Using a basting brush, brush generously with the butter mixture.

4. Bake in the preheated oven approximately 10 minutes, until lightly toasted. Remove from heat. Sprinkle with mozzarella cheese and any remaining butter mixture. Return to oven approximately 5 minutes, or until cheese is melted and bread is lightly browned.

BABA GHANOUSH
Servings: 12 | Prep: 5m | Cooks: 40m | Total: 3h45m

NUTRITION FACTS

Calories: 66 | Carbohydrates: 4.6g | Fat: 5.2g | Protein: 1.6g | Cholesterol: 0mg

INGREDIENTS

- 1 eggplant
- 1/4 cup lemon juice
- 1/4 cup tahini
- 2 tablespoons sesame seeds

- 2 cloves garlic, minced
- 2 cloves garlic, minced
- salt and pepper to taste
- 1 1/2 tablespoons olive oil

DIRECTIONS

1. Preheat oven to 400 degrees F (200 degrees C). Lightly grease a baking sheet.
2. Place eggplant on baking sheet, and make holes in the skin with a fork. Roast it for 30 to 40 minutes, turning occasionally, or until soft. Remove from oven, and place into a large bowl of cold water. Remove from water, and peel skin off.
3. Place eggplant, lemon juice, tahini, sesame seeds, and garlic in an electric blender, and puree. Season with salt and pepper to taste. Transfer eggplant mixture to a medium size mixing bowl, and slowly mix in olive oil. Refrigerate for 3 hours before serving.

MANGO SALSA
Servings: 8 | Prep: 15m | Cooks: 30m | Total: 45m

NUTRITION FACTS

Calories: 21 | Carbohydrates: 5.4g | Fat: 0.1g | Protein: 0.3g | Cholesterol: 0mg

INGREDIENTS

- 1 mango - peeled, seeded, and chopped
- 1/4 cup finely chopped red bell pepper
- 1 green onion, chopped
- 2 tablespoons chopped cilantro
- 1 fresh jalapeno chile pepper, finely chopped
- 2 tablespoons lime juice
- 1 tablespoon lemon juice

DIRECTIONS

1. In a medium bowl, mix mango, red bell pepper, green onion, cilantro, jalapeno, lime juice, and lemon juice. Cover, and allow to sit at least 30 minutes before serving.

VERONICA'S HOT SPINACH, ARTICHOKE AND CHILE DIP

Servings: 10 | Prep: 10m | Cooks: 30m | Total: 40m

NUTRITION FACTS

Calories: 314 | Carbohydrates: 7.8g | Fat: 28.8g | Protein: 9g | Cholesterol: 60mg

INGREDIENTS

- 2 (8 ounce) packages cream cheese, softened
- 1/2 cup mayonnaise
- 1 (4.5 ounce) can chopped green chiles, drained
- 1 cup freshly grated Parmesan cheese
- 1 (12 ounce) jar marinated artichoke hearts, drained and chopped
- 1/4 cup canned chopped jalapeno peppers, drained
- 1 (10 ounce) box frozen chopped spinach, thawed and drained

DIRECTIONS

1. Preheat oven to 350 degrees F (175 degrees C).
2. Mix together the cream cheese and mayonnaise in a bowl until smooth. Stir in the green chiles, Parmesan cheese, artichokes, peppers, and spinach. Spoon the mixture into a baking dish.
3. Bake in preheated oven until slightly browned, about 30 minutes.

TRADITIONAL FILIPINO LUMPIA

Servings: 15 | Prep: 45m | Cooks: 25m | Total: 1h10m

NUTRITION FACTS

Calories: 168 | Carbohydrates: 11g | Fat: 10.5g | Protein: 7g | Cholesterol: 23mg

INGREDIENTS

- 1 tablespoon vegetable oil
- 1 pound ground pork
- 2 cloves garlic, crushed
- 1/2 cup chopped onion
- 1/2 cup minced carrots
- 1/2 cup chopped green onions
- 1/2 cup thinly sliced green cabbage

- 1 teaspoon ground black pepper
- 1 teaspoon salt
- 1 teaspoon garlic powder
- 1 teaspoon soy sauce
- 30 lumpia wrappers
- 2 cups vegetable oil for frying

DIRECTIONS

1. Place a wok or large skillet over high heat, and pour in 1 tablespoon vegetable oil. Cook pork, stirring frequently, until no pink is showing. Remove pork from pan and set aside. Drain grease from pan, leaving a thin coating. Cook garlic and onion in the same pan for 2 minutes. Stir in the cooked pork, carrots, green onions, and cabbage. Season with pepper, salt, garlic powder, and soy sauce. Remove from heat, and set aside until cool enough to handle.

2. Place three heaping tablespoons of the filling diagonally near one corner of each wrapper, leaving a 1 1/2 inch space at both ends. Fold the side along the length of the filling over the filling, tuck in both ends, and roll neatly. Keep the roll tight as you assemble. Moisten the other side of the wrapper with water to seal the edge. Cover the rolls with plastic wrap to retain moisture.

3. Heat a heavy skillet over medium heat, add oil to 1/2 inch depth, and heat for 5 minutes. Slide 3 or 4 lumpia into the oil. Fry the rolls for 1 to 2 minutes, until all sides are golden brown. Drain on paper towels. Serve immediately.

GARLIC BREAD FANTASTIQUE
Servings: 6 | Prep: 10m | Cooks: 5m | Total: 15m

NUTRITION FACTS

Calories: 399 | Carbohydrates: 43.9g | Fat: 20.9g | Protein: 9.9g | Cholesterol: 44mg

INGREDIENTS

- 1/2 cup butter, softened
- 1/2 teaspoon salt

- 2 tablespoons mayonnaise
- 1/4 teaspoon sage
- 3 cloves garlic, chopped
- 2 teaspoons dried oregano
- 1/2 teaspoon black pepper
- 1 French baguette, halved lengthwise
- 2 tablespoons grated Parmesan cheese, or to taste

DIRECTIONS

1. Preheat oven to broil.
2. In a medium bowl combine butter, mayonnaise, sage, garlic, oregano, salt and pepper. Spread mixture evenly on bread and sprinkle with Parmesan cheese.
3. Place bread under broil for 5 minutes, or until lightly toasted.

PERFECT SUSHI RICE
Servings: 15 | Prep: 5m | Cooks: 20m | Total: 25m

NUTRITION FACTS

Calories: 112 | Carbohydrates: 23.5g | Fat: 1g | Protein: 1.7g | Cholesterol: 0mg

INGREDIENTS

- 2 cups uncooked glutinous white rice (sushi rice)
- 3 cups water
- 1/2 cup rice vinegar
- 1 tablespoon vegetable oil
- 1/4 cup white sugar
- 1 teaspoon salt

DIRECTIONS

1. Rinse the rice in a strainer or colander until the water runs clear. Combine with water in a medium saucepan. Bring to a boil, then reduce the heat to low, cover and cook for 20 minutes. Rice should be tender and water should be absorbed. Cool until cool enough to handle.
2. In a small saucepan, combine the rice vinegar, oil, sugar and salt. Cook over medium heat until the sugar dissolves. Cool, then stir into the cooked rice. When you pour this in to the rice it will seem very wet. Keep stirring and the rice will dry as it cools.

GRILLED PORTOBELLO MUSHROOMS
Servings: 3 | Prep: 10m | Cooks: 10m | Total: 1h20m

Calories: 217 | Carbohydrates: 11g | Fat: 19g | Protein: 3.2g | Cholesterol: 0mg

INGREDIENTS

- 3 portobello mushrooms
- 1/4 cup canola oil
- 3 tablespoons chopped onion
- 4 cloves garlic, minced
- 4 tablespoons balsamic vinegar

DIRECTIONS

1. Clean mushrooms and remove stems, reserve for other use. Place caps on a plate with the gills up.
2. In a small bowl, combine the oil, onion, garlic and vinegar. Pour mixture evenly over the mushroom caps and let stand for 1 hour.
3. Grill over hot grill for 10 minutes. Serve immediately.

JALAPENO POPPERS

Servings: 15 | Prep: 30m | Cooks: 30m | Total: 1h

NUTRITION FACTS

Calories: 187 | Carbohydrates: 9.8g | Fat: 13.8g | Protein: 6.5g | Cholesterol: 58mg

INGREDIENTS

- 1 (8 ounce) package cream cheese, softened
- 1 (8 ounce) package shredded sharp Cheddar cheese
- 1/4 cup mayonnaise
- 15 fresh jalapeno peppers, halved lengthwise and seeded
- 2 eggs, beaten
- 1/2 tablespoon milk
- 1 1/2 cups crushed corn flake cereal

DIRECTIONS

1. Preheat oven to 350 degrees F (175 degrees C). Lightly grease a medium baking sheet.
2. In a medium bowl, mix together cream cheese, sharp Cheddar cheese and mayonnaise. Stuff jalapeno halves with the mixture.
3. Whisk together eggs and milk in a small bowl. Place crushed corn flake cereal in a separate small bowl.

4. Dip each stuffed jalapeno half into the egg and milk mixture, then roll in corn flake cereal to coat.

5. Arrange in a single layer on the prepared baking sheet. Bake in the preheated oven 30 minutes, or until filling is bubbly and lightly browned.

MICROWAVE POPCORN
Servings: 3 | Prep: 2m | Cooks: 3m | Total: 5m

NUTRITION FACTS

Calories: 137 | Carbohydrates: 24.6g | Fat: 3.1g | Protein: 4.1g | Cholesterol: 0mg

INGREDIENTS

- 1/2 cup unpopped popcorn
- 1 teaspoon vegetable oil
- 1/2 teaspoon salt, or to taste

DIRECTIONS

1. In a cup or small bowl, mix together the unpopped popcorn and oil. Pour the coated corn into a brown paper lunch sack, and sprinkle in the salt. Fold the top of the bag over twice to seal in the ingredients.

2. Cook in the microwave at full power for 2 1/2 to 3 minutes, or until you hear pauses of about 2 seconds between pops. Carefully open the bag to avoid steam, and pour into a serving bowl.

MINI HAM AND CHEESE ROLLS
Servings: 24 | Prep: 15m | Cooks: 20m | Total: 35m | Servings: 24

NUTRITION FACTS

Calories: 145 | Carbohydrates: 10.2g | Fat: 9g | Protein: 5.7g | Cholesterol: 18mg

INGREDIENTS

- 2 tablespoons dried minced onion
- 1 tablespoon prepared mustard
- 2 tablespoons poppy seeds
- 1/2 cup margarine, melted
- 24 dinner rolls
- 1/2 pound chopped ham
- 1/2 pound thinly sliced Swiss cheese

DIRECTIONS

1. Preheat oven to 325 degrees F (165 degrees C).
2. In a small mixing bowl, combine onion flakes, mustard, poppy seeds and margarine.
3. Split each dinner roll. Make a sandwich of the ham and cheese and the dinner rolls. Arrange the sandwiches on a baking sheet. Drizzle the poppy seed mixture over the sandwiches.
4. Bake for 20 minutes, or until cheese has melted. Serve these sandwiches warm.

REUBEN DIP
Servings: 9 | Prep: 5m | Cooks: 25m | Total: 30m

NUTRITION FACTS

Calories: 393 | Carbohydrates: 7.3g | Fat: 31.7g | Protein: 20.9g | Cholesterol: 77mg

INGREDIENTS

- 1/2 cup mayonnaise
- 1/2 cup Thousand Island dressing
- 16 ounces sauerkraut, rinsed and squeezed dry
- 16 ounces shredded Swiss cheese
- 8 ounces shredded corned beef

DIRECTIONS

1. Preheat oven to 350 degrees F (175 degrees C).
2. In a small bowl, combine mayonnaise and dressing.
3. Spread sauerkraut into a 9x13-inch baking dish. Layer corned beef, Swiss cheese, and the mayonnaise-dressing mixture on top of the sauerkraut.
4. Bake for 20 to 25 minutes.

CRAB RANGOON
Servings: 15 | Prep: 25m | Cooks: 20m | Total: 45m

NUTRITION FACTS

Calories: 203 | Carbohydrates: 15.8g | Fat: 11.7g | Protein: 8.3g | Cholesterol: 39mg

INGREDIENTS

- 1 quart oil for deep frying
- 1 (8 ounce) package cream cheese, softened
- 2 (6 ounce) cans crabmeat, drained and flaked
- 1/4 teaspoon paprika
- 2 tablespoons water chestnuts, drained and chopped
- 1 (14 ounce) package wonton wrappers

- 1/2 teaspoon garlic powder

DIRECTIONS

1. In a large, heavy sauce pan heat oil to 375 degrees F (190 degrees C).
2. In a medium bowl, mix cream cheese, crabmeat, garlic powder, paprika and water chestnuts.
3. Place approximately 1 teaspoon of the cream cheese mixture in the center of wonton wrappers. Moisten wrapper edges with water, fold over the mixture and pinch to seal.
4. In small batches, fry the wontons 3 to 5 minutes, or until golden brown.

BACON AND CHEDDAR STUFFED MUSHROOMS
Servings: 8 | Prep: 15m | Cooks: 15m | Total: 30m

NUTRITION FACTS

Calories: 110 | Carbohydrates: 0.9g | Fat: 9.7g | Protein: 4.7g | Cholesterol: 22mg

INGREDIENTS

- 3 slices bacon
- 8 crimini mushrooms
- 1 tablespoon butter
- 1 tablespoon chopped onion
- 3/4 cup shredded Cheddar cheese

DIRECTIONS

1. Place bacon in a large, deep skillet. Cook over medium high heat until evenly brown. Drain, dice and set aside.
2. Preheat oven to 400 degrees F (200 degrees C).
3. Remove mushroom stems. Set aside caps. Chop the stems.
4. In a large saucepan over medium heat, melt the butter. Slowly cook and stir the chopped stems and onion until the onion is soft. Remove from heat.
5. In a medium bowl, stir together the mushroom stem mixture, bacon and 1/2 cup Cheddar. Mix well and scoop the mixture into the mushroom caps.
6. Bake in the preheated oven 15 minutes, or until the cheese has melted.
7. Remove the mushrooms from the oven, and sprinkle with the remaining cheese.

SAVORY CRAB STUFFED MUSHROOMS
Servings: 8 | Prep: 25m | Cooks: 20m | Total: 45m

NUTRITION FACTS

Calories: 176 | Carbohydrates: 7.3g | Fat: 11.8g | Protein: 9.8g | Cholesterol: 65mg

INGREDIENTS

- 3 tablespoons butter, melted
- 24 fresh mushrooms
- 2 tablespoons butter
- 2 tablespoons minced green onions
- 1 teaspoon lemon juice
- 1 cup diced cooked crabmeat

- 1/2 cup soft bread crumbs
- 1 egg, beaten
- 1/2 teaspoon dried dill weed
- 3/4 cup shredded Monterey Jack cheese, divided
- 1/4 cup dry white wine

DIRECTIONS

1. Preheat oven to 400 degrees F (200 degrees C). Prepare a 9x13 inch baking dish with 3 tablespoons butter.
2. Remove stems from mushrooms. Set aside caps. Finely chop stems.
3. Melt 2 tablespoons butter in a medium saucepan over medium heat. Stir in the chopped stems and green onions and cook until soft, about 3 minutes. Remove saucepan from heat. Stir in lemon juice, crabmeat, soft bread crumbs, egg, dill weed and 1/4 cup Monterey Jack cheese. Thoroughly blend the mixture.
4. Place mushroom caps in the buttered pan, and stir until caps are coated with the butter. Arrange caps cavity side up, and stuff cavities generously with the green onion and crabmeat mixture. Top with remaining Monterey Jack cheese. Pour wine into the pan around the mushrooms.
5. Bake uncovered in the preheated oven 15 to 20 minutes, until cheese is melted and lightly browned. Serve warm.

ROCKIN' SALSA
Servings: 64 | Prep: 45m | Cooks: 3h20m | Total: 6h5m

NUTRITION FACTS

Calories: 25 | Carbohydrates: 5.9g | Fat: 0.2g | Protein: 0.9g | Cholesterol: 0mg

INGREDIENTS

- 1 red onion, chopped
- 1 white onion, chopped

- 1/2 cup white vinegar
- 2 tablespoons garlic powder

- 1 yellow onion, chopped
- 6 pounds fresh tomatoes, peeled and chopped
- 2 banana peppers, chopped
- 3 green bell peppers, chopped
- 1/4 cup white sugar
- 3 (6 ounce) cans tomato paste
- 1 1/2 tablespoons salt
- 1 tablespoon cayenne pepper
- 1 1/2 teaspoons ground cumin
- 1/4 cup brown sugar
- 8 pint canning jars with lids and rings

DIRECTIONS

1. Combine red onion, white onion, yellow onion, tomatoes, banana peppers, green peppers, tomato paste, white vinegar, garlic powder, salt, cayenne pepper, cumin, brown sugar, and white sugar in a large pot. Simmer until thick, about 3 hours.

2. Sterilize the jars and lids in boiling water for at least 5 minutes. Pack the salsa into the hot, sterilized jars, filling the jars to within 1/4 inch of the top. Run a knife or a thin spatula around the insides of the jars after they have been filled to remove any air bubbles. Wipe the rims of the jars with a moist paper towel to remove any food residue. Top with lids, and screw on rings.

3. Place a rack in the bottom of a large stockpot and fill halfway with water. Bring to a boil over high heat, then carefully lower the jars into the pot using a holder. Leave a 2 inch space between the jars. Pour in more boiling water if necessary until the water level is at least 1 inch above the tops of the jars. Bring the water to a full boil, cover the pot, and process for 10 to 15 minutes.

4. Remove the jars from the stockpot and place onto a cloth-covered or wood surface, several inches apart, until cool. Once cool, press the top of each lid with a finger, ensuring that the seal is tight (lid does not move up or down at all). Refrigerate after opening.

ESPINACAS CON GARBANZOS
Servings: 4 | Prep: 15m | Cooks: 10m | Total: 25m

NUTRITION FACTS

Calories: 169 | Carbohydrates: 26g | Fat: 4.9g | Protein: 7.3g | Cholesterol: 0mg

INGREDIENTS

- 1 tablespoon extra-virgin olive oil
- 4 cloves garlic, minced
- 1/2 onion, diced
- 1 (10 ounce) box frozen chopped spinach, thawed and drained well
- 1 (12 ounce) can garbanzo beans, drained
- 1/2 teaspoon cumin
- 1/2 teaspoon salt

DIRECTIONS

1. Heat the olive oil in a skillet over medium-low heat. Cook the garlic and onion in the oil until translucent, about 5 minutes. Stir in the spinach, garbanzo beans, cumin, and salt. Use your stirring spoon to lightly mash the beans as the mixture cooks. Allow to cook until thoroughly heated.

BUFFALO CHICKEN WINGS
Servings: 8 | Prep: 10m | Cooks: 15m | Total: 25m

NUTRITION FACTS

Calories: 256 | Carbohydrates: 0.2g | Fat: 23.9g | Protein: 10g | Cholesterol: 46mg

INGREDIENTS

- 1 quart vegetable oil for deep frying
- 24 chicken wings, tips removed and wings cut in half at joint
- 4 tablespoons butter

- 1 tablespoon distilled white vinegar
- 5 tablespoons hot pepper sauce
- salt and pepper to taste

DIRECTIONS

1. Heat the oil in a large skillet or deep fryer to 375 degrees F (190 degrees C). Deep fry chicken wings in oil until done, about 10 minutes. Remove chicken from skillet or deep fryer and drain on paper towels..

2. Melt the butter in a large skillet. Stir in the, vinegar and hot pepper sauce. Season with salt and pepper to taste. Add cooked chicken to sauce and stir over low heat to coat. The longer the wings simmer in the sauce, the hotter they will be. Serve warm.

SPINACH AND ARTICHOKE DIP
Servings: 6 | Prep: 10m | Cooks: 15m | Total: 25m

NUTRITION FACTS

Calories: 559 | Carbohydrates: 11.1g | Fat: 48.4g | Protein: 22.3g | Cholesterol: 71mg

INGREDIENTS

- 1 (14 ounce) can artichoke hearts, drained and chopped
- 1 (10 ounce) package frozen chopped spinach, thawed and drained

- 1 cup grated Parmesan cheese
- 2 1/2 cups shredded Monterey Jack cheese

- 1 cup mayonnaise

DIRECTIONS

1. Preheat oven to 350 degrees F (175 degrees C). Lightly grease a 1 quart baking dish.
2. In a medium bowl, mix together artichoke hearts, spinach, mayonnaise, Parmesan cheese and 2 cups Monterey Jack cheese. Transfer mixture to the prepared baking dish, and sprinkle with remaining 1/2 cup of Monterey Jack cheese.
3. Bake in the center of the preheated oven until the cheese is melted, about 15 minutes.

MEXICAN CREAM CHEESE ROLLUPS
Servings: 8 | Prep: 5m | Cooks: 1h | Total: 1h5m

NUTRITION FACTS

Calories: 428 | Carbohydrates: 43.5g | Fat: 19.4g | Protein: 9.1g | Cholesterol: 34mg

INGREDIENTS

- 1 (8 ounce) package cream cheese, softened
- 1/3 cup mayonnaise
- 2/3 cup pitted green olives, chopped
- 1 (2.25 ounce) can black olives, chopped
- 6 green onions, chopped
- 8 (10 inch) flour tortillas
- 1/2 cup salsa

DIRECTIONS

1. In a medium bowl, mix together cream cheese, mayonnaise, green olives, black olives and green onions.
2. Spread cream cheese mixture in a thin layer onto each tortilla. Roll up tortillas. Chill about 1 hour, or until the filling is firm.
3. Slice chilled rollups into 1 inch pieces. Serve with salsa for dipping.

WARM CRAB PARMESAN DIP
Servings: 40 | Prep: 10m | Cooks: 45m | Total: 55m

NUTRITION FACTS

Calories: 88 | Carbohydrates: 0.8g | Fat: 8.4g | Protein: 2.5g | Cholesterol: 16mg

INGREDIENTS

- 1 (4.5 ounce) can crabmeat, drained
- 1 (8 ounce) package cream cheese, softened
- 1 cup mayonnaise

- 1 1/2 cups grated Parmesan cheese
- 1 cup sour cream
- 4 cloves garlic, peeled and crushed (or to taste)

DIRECTIONS

1. Preheat oven to 350 degrees F (175 degrees C).
2. In a small baking dish, mix the crabmeat, cream cheese, mayonnaise, Parmesan cheese, sour cream and garlic.
3. Bake uncovered in the preheated oven until bubbly and lightly browned, about 45 minutes.

ZESTY PORCUPINE MEATBALLS
Servings: 5 | Prep: 20m | Cooks: 20m | Total: 40m

NUTRITION FACTS

Calories: 408 | Carbohydrates: 32.4g | Fat: 21.6g | Protein: 20.6g | Cholesterol: 105mg

INGREDIENTS

- 1 egg
- 2 (10.75 ounce) cans condensed tomato soup
- 1/4 cup instant rice
- 1/4 cup chopped onion
- 1/4 cup Worcestershire sauce

- 1 tablespoon chopped fresh parsley
- 1 teaspoon onion salt
- 1/4 teaspoon ground black pepper
- 1 pound lean ground beef

DIRECTIONS

1. Lightly beat egg with a fork, then add a heaping tablespoon of the soup and mix lightly. Mix in rice, onion, parsley, onion salt and pepper. Stir in the ground beef and mix well with hands. From mixture into 1 1/2 inch round meatballs.
2. Coat a large skillet over medium heat with cooking spray. Cook meatballs and brown on all sides.
3. Combine remaining soup with Worcestershire (you can increase or decrease Worcestershire to your liking), stir until smooth, then spoon over meatballs. Cover with lid and simmer for 20 to 30 minutes, stirring every few minutes.

CANDIED ALMONDS

Servings: 8 | Prep: 5m | Cooks: 15m | Total: 35m

NUTRITION FACTS

Calories: 304 | Carbohydrates: 32.7g | Fat: 18g | Protein: 7.6g | Cholesterol: 0mg

INGREDIENTS

- 1/2 cup water
- 1 cup white sugar
- 1 tablespoon ground cinnamon
- 2 cups whole almonds

DIRECTIONS

1. Combine the water, sugar, and cinnamon in a saucepan over medium heat; bring to a boil; add the almonds. Cook and stir the mixture until the liquid evaporates and leaves a syrup-like coating on the almonds. Pour the almonds onto a baking sheet lined with waxed paper. Separate almonds using forks. Allow to cool about 15 minutes.

BABY BLT

Servings: 24 | Prep: 20m | Cooks: 10m | Total: 1h30m | Additional: 1h

NUTRITION FACTS

Calories: 71 | Carbohydrates: 1.1g | Fat: 6.3g | Protein: 2.5g | Cholesterol: 9mg

INGREDIENTS

- 1 pound bacon, cooked and crumbled
- 1/2 cup mayonnaise
- 1/4 cup green onions, chopped
- 2 tablespoons chopped fresh parsley
- 24 cherry tomatoes

DIRECTIONS

1. Place bacon in a large, deep skillet. Cook over medium high heat for 6 to 8 minutes, or until evenly brown. Once cooled, crumble and set aside.
2. In a bowl, stir together the mayonnaise, bacon, green onions, and parsley until well blended. Set aside.

3. Cut a small slice from the top of each tomato. Using a melon baller or small spoon, scoop out the inside of each tomato and discard. Fill each tomato with the bacon mixture, and refrigerate for 1 hour. Serve chilled.

ARTICHOKE BRUSCHETTA
Servings: 8 | Prep: 18m | Cooks: 2m | Total: 20m

NUTRITION FACTS

Calories: 278 | Carbohydrates: 35.7g | Fat: 11.1g | Protein: 10g | Cholesterol: 11mg

INGREDIENTS

- 1 (6.5 ounce) jar marinated artichoke hearts, drained and chopped
- 1/2 cup grated Romano cheese
- 1/3 cup finely chopped red onion
- 5 tablespoons mayonnaise
- 1 French baguette, cut into 1/3 inch thick slices

DIRECTIONS

1. Preheat the broiler.
2. In a medium bowl, mix marinated artichoke hearts, Romano cheese, red onion and mayonnaise. Top French baguette slices with equal amounts of the artichoke heart mixture. Arrange slices in a single layer on a large baking sheet.
3. Broil in the preheated oven 2 minutes, or until toppings are bubbly and lightly browned.

DIP FOR THE STARS
Servings: 30 | Prep: 20m | Cooks: 1h | Total: 1h20m

NUTRITION FACTS

Calories: 162 | Carbohydrates: 2.9g | Fat: 15.2g | Protein: 4.2g | Cholesterol: 36mg

INGREDIENTS

- 1 cup unsalted butter
- 3/4 pound feta cheese, crumbled
- 1 (8 ounce) package cream cheese, softened
- ground white pepper, to taste
- 1 cup chopped sun-dried tomatoes
- 2 cloves garlic, minced
- 1 shallot, minced
- 3 tablespoons dry vermouth
- 1/2 cup pine nuts, toasted
- 3/4 cup pesto sauce

DIRECTIONS

1. In a food processor, combine the butter, feta cheese, cream cheese, garlic, shallot, vermouth, and white pepper. Process until smooth.
2. Oil a medium bowl, or gelatin mold, and line with plastic wrap for easy removal. Layer the dip into the mold as follows: Sun-dried tomatoes, pine nuts, pesto, cheese mixture. Repeat. Pat down into the mold, and refrigerate for at least one hour.
3. Turn the dip out onto a serving plate, and remove plastic wrap. Serve with crackers.

MEXICAN SHRIMP COCKTAIL
Servings: 6 | Prep: 15m | Cooks: 3h | Total: 3h15m

NUTRITION FACTS

Calories: 258 | Carbohydrates: 15.8g | Fat: 6.7g| Protein: 33.3g | Cholesterol: 295mg

INGREDIENTS

- 2 pounds cooked shrimp, peeled and deveined
- 1 tablespoon crushed garlic
- 1/2 cup finely chopped red onion
- 1/4 cup fresh cilantro, chopped
- salt to taste
- 1 1/2 cups tomato and clam juice cocktail

- 1/4 cup ketchup
- 1/4 cup fresh lime juice
- 1 teaspoon hot pepper sauce, or to taste
- 1/4 cup prepared horseradish
- 1 ripe avocado - peeled, pitted and chopped

DIRECTIONS

1. Place the shrimp in a large bowl. Stir garlic, red onion, and cilantro. Mix in tomato and clam juice cocktail, ketchup, lime juice, hot pepper sauce, and horseradish. Season with salt. Gently stir in avocado. Cover, and refrigerate 2 to 3 hours. Serve in one large bowl or ladle into individual bowl.

FETA CHEESE FOLDOVERS
Servings: 12 | Prep: 20m | Cooks: 20m | Total: 40m

NUTRITION FACTS

Calories: 286 | Carbohydrates: 19.4g | Fat: 20.4g | Protein: 6.4g | Cholesterol: 49mg

INGREDIENTS

- 8 ounces feta cheese, crumbled

- 3 tablespoons finely chopped green onions

- 1 egg, beaten

- 1 (17.5 ounce) package frozen puff pastry, thawed

- 1 egg yolk, beaten with 1 teaspoon water

DIRECTIONS

1. Preheat oven to 375 degrees F (190 degrees C).

2. In a small bowl, blend feta cheese, green onions, and egg. Cut pastry into 12 (3 inch) squares. Place a mounded tablespoon of feta mixture in the center of each square. Moisten edges with water, and fold pastry over filling to form a triangle. Press edges together firmly with a fork to seal. Lightly brush pastries with the egg yolk mixture.

3. Bake for 20 minutes in the preheated oven, or until golden brown. Serve warm or at room temperature.

TOASTED PUMPKIN SEEDS WITH SUGAR AND SPICE
Servings: 4 | Prep: 15m | Cooks: 45m | Total: 1h

NUTRITION FACTS

Calories: 290 | Carbohydrates: 25g | Fat: 19.3g | Protein: 8.5g | Cholesterol: 0mg

INGREDIENTS

- 1 cup raw pumpkin seeds, rinsed and dried

- 6 tablespoons white sugar, divided

- 1/4 teaspoon salt

- 1/2 teaspoon pumpkin pie spice

- 1 tablespoon vegetable oil

DIRECTIONS

1. Preheat the oven to 250 degrees F (120 degrees C). Spread pumpkin seeds in a single layer on a baking sheet. Toast for 45 minutes, stirring occasionally, until dry and toasted. Larger seeds may take longer.

2. In a large bowl, stir together 2 tablespoons of white sugar, salt, and pumpkin pie spice. Set aside. Heat the oil in a large skillet over medium-high heat. Add the pumpkin seeds and sprinkle the

remaining sugar over them. Stir with a wooden spoon until the sugar melts, about 45 seconds. Pour seeds into the bowl with the spiced sugar and stir until coated. Allow to cool before serving. Store in an airtight container at room temperature.

DINAH'S STUFFED MUSHROOMS
Servings: 10 | Prep: 20m | Cooks: 30m | Total: 50m

NUTRITION FACTS

Calories: 383 | Carbohydrates: 11.2g | Fat: 31.3g | Protein: 15.5g | Cholesterol: 106mg

INGREDIENTS

- 20 fresh mushrooms, stems removed
- 2 (6.5 ounce) cans minced clams, drained
- 3/4 cup dry bread crumbs
- 1/2 cup chopped green bell pepper
- ground black pepper to taste
- 2 cloves garlic, peeled and minced
- 1/2 cup grated Parmesan cheese
- 1 small onion, finely chopped
- 2 tablespoons dried parsley
- 2 tablespoons Italian-style seasoning
- 1 1/2 cups butter, melted
- 1/2 cup shredded mozzarella cheese

DIRECTIONS

1. Preheat oven to 350 degrees F (175 degrees C). Lightly grease a 9x13 inch baking dish.
2. Arrange mushroom caps hollow side up in the baking dish.
3. In a medium bowl, mix together minced clams, garlic, Parmesan cheese, onion, bread crumbs, green bell pepper, parsley, Italian-style seasoning and black pepper. Slowly stir in approximately 1/2 the butter, enough to make the mixture slightly moist.
4. Generously fill the mushroom caps with the clam mixture. Sprinkle with mozzarella cheese. Drizzle with remaining butter.
5. Bake in the preheated oven 30 minutes, or until lightly browned.

MARYLAND CRAB CAKES
Servings: 4 | Prep: 15m | Cooks: 20m | Total: 35m

NUTRITION FACTS

Calories: 211 | Carbohydrates: 2.6g | Fat: 13g | Protein: 20.1g | Cholesterol: 185mg

INGREDIENTS

- 1 pound crabmeat, shredded
- 1 1/2 tablespoons dry bread crumbs
- 2 teaspoons chopped fresh parsley
- salt and pepper to taste
- 1 egg
- 1 1/2 tablespoons mayonnaise
- 1/2 teaspoon ground dry mustard
- 1 dash hot pepper sauce

DIRECTIONS

1. Preheat oven broiler.
2. Mix together crabmeat, bread crumbs, parsley, salt and pepper.
3. Beat together egg, mayonnaise, hot sauce and mustard. Combine with other ingredients and mix well. Form into patties and place on a lightly greased broiler pan or baking sheet.
4. Broil for 10 to 15 minutes, until lightly brown.

BACON WATER CHESTNUT ROLLS
Servings: 24 | Prep: 10m | Cooks: 1h | Total: 1h010m

NUTRITION FACTS

Calories: 85 | Carbohydrates: 6.5g | Fat: 3.1g | Protein: 1.3g | Cholesterol: 7mg

INGREDIENTS

- 1 (8 ounce) can water chestnuts, halved
- 1/2 pound sliced bacon, cut in half
- 1/4 cup mayonnaise
- 1/2 cup packed light brown sugar
- 1/4 cup tomato-based chili sauce

DIRECTIONS

1. Preheat oven to 350 degrees F (175 degrees C).
2. Wrap each water chestnut with a piece of bacon. Place the rolls seam-side down in a baking dish.
3. Bake in the preheated oven for 30 minutes, or until bacon is crisp and cooked through. Drain off the grease. In a small bowl, stir together the mayonnaise, brown sugar and chili sauce; pour over the bacon-chestnut rolls. Return to the oven and bake for another 30 minutes.

DETROIT HOT HONEY WINGS
Servings: 6 | Prep: 15m | Cooks: 20m | Total: 35m

NUTRITION FACTS

Calories: 420 | Carbohydrates: 47.1g | Fat: 22.8g | Protein: 10.6g | Cholesterol: 72mg

INGREDIENTS

- 2 pounds chicken wings, tips discarded
- 1 teaspoon cayenne pepper (add more if you can stand it)
- salt and ground black pepper to taste
- 1 cup honey
- 1/2 cup butter, melted
- 1/2 cup hot sauce

DIRECTIONS

1. Preheat an outdoor grill for medium heat and lightly oil grate.
2. Wash the wings well and pat dry with paper towel. Season the meat with cayenne, salt, and pepper.
3. Cook the chicken wings on preheated grill until cooked through and juices run clear, 20 to 30 minutes depending on the size of the wings. Brush the wings liberally using 1/2 cup of honey while they are cooking.
4. Melt the butter, pour into a large bowl and mix in the remaining 1/2 cup of honey and hot sauce. Remove the wings from the grill and immediately toss them in the hot honey butter sauce to coat. Serve the wings 'wet' or return them to the grill for 1 minute per side to set the sauce.

BACON-WRAPPED JALAPENO POPPERS

Servings: 6 | Prep: 15m | Cooks: 15m | Total: 30m

NUTRITION FACTS

Calories: 213 | Carbohydrates: 2.5g | Fat: 17.7g | Protein: 11g | Cholesterol: 51mg

INGREDIENTS

- 1/2 cup cream cheese
- 1/2 cup shredded sharp Cheddar cheese
- 12 jalapeno peppers, halved lengthwise, seeds and membranes removed
- 12 slices bacon

DIRECTIONS

1. Preheat oven to 400 degrees F (200 degrees C). Line a baking sheet with aluminum foil.
2. Mix cream cheese and Cheddar cheese together in a bowl until evenly blended. Fill each jalapeno half with the cheese mixture. Put halves back together and wrap each stuffed pepper with a slice of bacon. Arrange bacon-wrapped peppers on the prepared baking sheet.
3. Bake in the preheated oven until bacon is crispy, about 15 minutes.

SPICY HOT CHICKEN LEGS

Servings: 6 | Prep: 5m | Cooks: 3h | Total: 3h5m

NUTRITION FACTS

Calories: 685 | Carbohydrates: 5g | Fat: 55.6g | Protein: 41.4g | Cholesterol: 159mg

INGREDIENTS

- 12 chicken drumsticks
- 1 (5 ounce) bottle hot red pepper sauce
- 1/4 cup butter, cubed
- 1/2 teaspoon garlic powder
- 1/2 teaspoon onion powder
- salt and pepper to taste
- 1 1/2 cups blue cheese salad dressing

DIRECTIONS

1. Place the drumsticks in a slow cooker, and sprinkle evenly with pieces of butter. Pour the hot sauce over the chicken, then season with garlic powder, onion powder, salt and pepper. Cover, and cook on High for 3 hours, or until tender. Serve chicken legs with blue cheese dressing on the side.

BAKED PORK SPRING ROLLS

Servings: 12 | Prep: 25m | Cooks: 20m | Total: 45m

NUTRITION FACTS

Calories: 154 | Carbohydrates: 20.1g | Fat: 4.9g | Protein: 6.7g | Cholesterol: 15mg

INGREDIENTS

- 1/2 pound ground pork
- 1 cup finely shredded cabbage
- 1/4 cup finely shredded carrot
- 2 green onions, thinly sliced
- 2 tablespoons chopped fresh cilantro
- 1 tablespoon water
- 4 teaspoons vegetable oil
- 1/2 teaspoon sesame oil
- 1/2 tablespoon oyster sauce
- 2 teaspoons grated fresh ginger root
- 1 1/2 teaspoons minced garlic
- 1 teaspoon chile sauce
- 12 (7 inch square) spring roll wrappers
-

DIRECTIONS

1. Preheat oven to 425 degrees F (220 degrees C).
2. Place pork in a medium saucepan. Cook over medium high heat until evenly brown. Remove from heat and drain.
3. In a medium bowl, mix together pork, cabbage, carrot, green onions, cilantro, sesame oil, oyster sauce, ginger, garlic and chile sauce.
4. Mix cornstarch and water in a small bowl.
5. Place approximately 1 tablespoon of the pork mixture in the center of spring roll wrappers. Roll wrappers around the mixture, folding edges inward to close. Moisten fingers in the cornstarch and water mixture, and brush wrapper seams to seal.
6. Arrange spring rolls in a single layer on a medium baking sheet. Brush with vegetable oil. Bake in the preheated oven 20 minutes, until hot and lightly browned. For crispier spring rolls, turn after 10 minutes.

CANDY COATED PECANS
Servings: 10 | Prep: 10m | Cooks: 15m | Total: 25m

NUTRITION FACTS

Calories: 342 | Carbohydrates: 16.8g | Fat: 31.1g | Protein: 4.3g | Cholesterol: 0mg

INGREDIENTS

- 1 egg white
- 1/2 cup packed brown sugar

- 1 dash vanilla extract
- 4 cups pecans

DIRECTIONS

1. Preheat oven to 275 degrees F (135 degrees C). Line a cookie sheet with wax paper. Spray the wax paper with cooking spray.
2. Beat egg white until stiff. Add brown sugar and vanilla. Stir until smooth. Mix in pecans and stir until coated. Pour the nuts onto the prepared cookie sheet.
3. Bake until browned, approximately 10 to 15 minutes.

MARY'S ROASTED RED PEPPER DIP
Servings: 32 | Prep: 10m | Cooks: 20m | Total: 30m

NUTRITION FACTS

Calories: 116 | Carbohydrates: 1g | Fat: 11.1g | Protein: 3.3g | Cholesterol: 20mg

INGREDIENTS

- 1 (7 ounce) jar roasted red peppers, drained and diced
- 3/4 pound shredded Monterey Jack cheese
- 1 (8 ounce) package cream cheese, softened
- 1 cup mayonnaise
- 1 tablespoon minced onion
- 1 clove garlic, minced
- 2 tablespoons prepared Dijon-style mustard

DIRECTIONS

1. Preheat oven to 350 degrees F (175 degrees C).
2. In a small baking dish, mix the roasted red peppers, Monterey Jack cheese, cream cheese, mayonnaise, onion, garlic and Dijon-style mustard.
3. Bake in the preheated oven 20 minutes, or until bubbly and lightly browned. Serve warm.

SWEET, SALTY, SPICY PARTY NUTS
Servings: 16 | Prep: 10m | Cooks: 17m | Total: 27m

NUTRITION FACTS

Calories: 219 | Carbohydrates: 12.7g | Fat: 18.1g | Protein: 4.8g | Cholesterol: 2mg

INGREDIENTS

- Cooking spray
- 1 cup untoasted walnut halves
- 1 cup untoasted pecan halves
- 1 cup unsalted, dry roasted almonds
- 1 cup unsalted, dry roasted cashews
- 1 teaspoon salt
- 1/2 teaspoon freshly ground black pepper
- 1/4 teaspoon ground cumin
- 1/4 teaspoon cayenne pepper
- 1/2 cup white sugar
- 1/4 cup water
- 1 tablespoon butter

DIRECTIONS

1. Preheat oven to 350 degrees F (175 degrees C). Line a baking sheet with aluminum foil and lightly coat with cooking spray.
2. Combine walnut halves, pecan halves, almonds, and cashews in a large bowl. Add salt, black pepper, cumin, and cayenne pepper; toss to coat.
3. Heat sugar, water, and butter in a small saucepan over medium heat until the butter is melted. Cook for 1 minute and remove from heat. Slowly pour butter mixture over the bowl of nuts and stir to coat.
4. Transfer nuts to the prepared baking sheet and spread into a single layer.
5. Bake nuts in the preheated oven for 10 minutes. Stir nuts until the warm syrup coats every nut. Spread into a single layer, return to the oven, and bake until nuts are sticky and roasted, about 6 minutes. Allow to cool before serving.

KING CRAB APPETIZERS
Servings: 12 | Prep: 10m | Cooks: 20m | Total: 30m

NUTRITION FACTS

Calories: 299 | Carbohydrates: 25.1g | Fat: 18g | Protein: 9.6g | Cholesterol: 40mg

INGREDIENTS

- 2 (12 ounce) packages refrigerated biscuit dough
- 1 (8 ounce) package cream cheese, softened
- 1 (6 ounce) can crab meat, drained
- 2 tablespoons mayonnaise
- 1 pinch paprika
- 2 tablespoons grated Parmesan cheese
- 1/2 cup shredded Cheddar cheese
- 2 tablespoons thinly sliced green onion
- 1 teaspoon Worcestershire sauce

DIRECTIONS

1. Preheat oven to 375 degrees F (190 degrees C). Lightly grease 12 tartlet pans.
2. Divide rolls in half and press into the prepared tartlet pans. Set aside.
3. In a large bowl, combine cream cheese, crab, mayonnaise, Parmesan cheese, Cheddar cheese, green onions and Worcestershire sauce. Spoon 1 teaspoon of mixture into tarts and garnish with paprika.
4. Bake at 375 degrees F (190 degrees C) for 15 to 20 minutes, or until light brown. These freeze wonderfully. Just reheat before serving.

RESTAURANT-STYLE POTATO SKINS
Servings: 6 | Prep: 30m | Cooks: 7m | Total: 37m

NUTRITION FACTS

Calories: 519 | Carbohydrates: 40.9g | Fat: 32.8g | Protein: 17.1g | Cholesterol: 75mg

INGREDIENTS

- 6 potatoes
- 1 cup vegetable oil
- 8 ounces shredded Cheddar cheese
- 1/8 cup bacon bits
- 1 (16 ounce) container sour cream

DIRECTIONS

1. Preheat oven to 375 degrees F (190 degrees C). Lightly grease a 9x13 inch baking pan.
2. Pierce potatoes with a fork. Microwave the potatoes on high until they are soft; approximately 10 to 12 minutes.
3. Cut the potatoes in half vertically. Scoop the inside out of the potatoes, until 1/4 inch of the potato shell remains.
4. Heat oil to 365 degrees F (180 degrees C) in a deep fryer or a deep saucepan. Place the potatoes in hot oil, fry for 5 minutes. Drain potatoes on paper towels.
5. Fill the potato shells with cheese and bacon bits. Arrange them in the prepared baking pan.
6. Bake for 7 minutes, or until the cheese is melted. Serve hot with sour cream.

COCKTAIL MEATBALLS
Servings: 8 | Prep: 25m | Cooks: 40m | Total: 1h10m

NUTRITION FACTS

Calories: 458 | Carbohydrates: 52.5g | Fat: 22.8g | Protein: 12.7g | Cholesterol: 72mg

INGREDIENTS

- 1 pound ground beef
- 1/2 cup dried bread crumbs
- 1/3 cup chopped onion
- 1/4 cup milk
- 1 egg
- 1 teaspoon salt
- 1/2 teaspoon Worcestershire sauce
- 1/8 teaspoon ground black pepper
- 1/4 cup shortening
- 12 fluid ounces tomato-based chili sauce
- 1 1/4 cups grape jelly

DIRECTIONS

1. In a large bowl, combine ground beef, bread crumbs, onion, milk, egg, salt, Worcestershire sauce, and ground black pepper. Mix together, and shape into meatballs.

2. In a large skillet, heat shortening over medium heat. Add meatballs, and cook until browned, about 5 to 7 minutes. Remove from skillet, and drain on paper towels.

3. Add chili sauce and jelly to skillet; heat, stirring, until jelly is melted. Return meatballs to skillet, and stir until coated. Reduce heat to low. Simmer, uncovered, for 30 minutes.

CHEESE BALL

Servings: 32 | Prep: 15m | Cooks: 2h | Total: 2h15m

NUTRITION FACTS

Calories: 149 | Carbohydrates: 1.9g | Fat: 14g | Protein: 4.8g | Cholesterol: 28mg

INGREDIENTS

- 2 (8 ounce) packages cream cheese, softened
- 3 1/2 cups shredded sharp Cheddar cheese
- 1 (1 ounce) package Ranch-style dressing mix
- 12 cups chopped pecans
- 4 pecan halves

DIRECTIONS

1. In a large bowl, mix together cream cheese, Cheddar cheese, and dressing mix. Form into one large ball or two smaller balls. Roll in chopped pecans to coat surface. Decorate the top with pecan halves. Refrigerate for at least 2 hours, or overnight.

TACO BAKE

Servings: 8 | Prep: 15m | Cooks: 25m | Total: 40m

NUTRITION FACTS

Calories: 413 | Carbohydrates: 15.4g | Fat: 26.9g | Protein: 25.9g | Cholesterol: 93mg

INGREDIENTS

- 1 1/2 pounds lean ground beef
- 1 (1.25 ounce) package taco seasoning mix
- 1 (16 ounce) can refried beans
- 1 (16 ounce) jar salsa
- 2 cups shredded Monterey Jack cheese

DIRECTIONS

1. Preheat oven to 325 degrees F (160 degrees C).
2. In a large, heavy skillet over medium-high heat, brown ground beef, and drain fat. Mix in dry taco seasoning.

3. Spoon browned meat into a 9x13 inch glass baking dish. Spoon a layer of refried beans over meat, then salsa. Top with shredded cheese.

4. Bake about 20 to 25 minutes in the preheated oven.

GRANOLA BARS
Servings: 20 | Prep: 15m | Cooks: 25m | Total: 40m

NUTRITION FACTS

Calories: 212 | Carbohydrates: 32.2g | Fat: 8.6g | Protein: 3.4g | Cholesterol: 9mg

INGREDIENTS

- 2 cups quick cooking oats
- 1 cup all-purpose flour
- 3/4 cup packed brown sugar
- 3/4 cup raisins
- 1/2 cup wheat germ
- 1 egg

- 1/2 teaspoon salt
- 1/2 teaspoon ground cinnamon
- 1/2 cup chopped English walnuts
- 1/2 cup vegetable oil
- 1/2 cup honey
- 2 teaspoons vanilla extract

DIRECTIONS

1. Preheat oven to 350 degrees F (175 degrees C). Line a 9x13 inch baking pan with aluminum foil or parchment paper, and spray with vegetable oil spray.

2. In a large bowl, stir together oats, flour, brown sugar, raisins, wheat germ, salt, cinnamon, and walnuts. In a smaller bowl, thoroughly blend oil, honey, egg, and vanilla; pour into the flour mixture, and mix by hand until the liquid is evenly distributed. Press evenly into the prepared baking pan.

3. Bake 25 to 30 minutes in the preheated oven, or until the edges are golden. Cool completely in pan before turning out onto a cutting board and cutting into bars.

STUFFED JALAPENOS
Servings: 8 | Prep: 20m | Cooks: 45m | Total: 1h5m

NUTRITION FACTS

Calories: 186 | Carbohydrates: 1.9g | Fat: 18g | Protein: 4.3g | Cholesterol: 37mg

INGREDIENTS

- 12 fresh jalapeno peppers, halved lengthwise and seeded
- 1 (8 ounce) package whipped cream cheese
- 12 slices bacon, cut in half

DIRECTIONS

1. Preheat oven to 400 degrees F (200 degrees C).
2. Stuff each jalapeno half with whipped cream cheese. Wrap a half slice of bacon around each stuffed jalapeno half.
3. Arrange wrapped jalapeno halves in a single layer on a medium baking sheet. Bake in the preheated oven 45 minutes, or until bacon is evenly browned and crisp.

HONEY MUSTARD SAUCE
Servings: 18| Prep: 10m | Cooks: 2h | Total: 2h10m

NUTRITION FACTS

Calories: 164 | Carbohydrates: 9g | Fat: 14.6g | Protein: 0.2g | Cholesterol: 7mg

INGREDIENTS

- 1 1/2 cups mayonnaise
- 1/4 cup prepared Dijon-style mustard
- 1/2 cup honey

DIRECTIONS

1. In a medium bowl, blend the mayonnaise, Dijon-style mustard and honey. Chill in the refrigerator at least 2 hours before serving.

AVOCADO CORN SALSA
Servings: 32 | Prep: 30m | Cooks: 8h | Total: 8h30m

NUTRITION FACTS

Calories: 81| Carbohydrates: 6.1g | Fat: 6.5g | Protein: 1.1g | Cholesterol: 0mg

INGREDIENTS

- 1 (16 ounce) package frozen corn kernels, thawed
- 1/4 cup lemon juice

- 2 (2.25 ounce) cans sliced ripe olives, drained
- 1 red bell pepper, chopped
- 1 small onion, chopped
- 5 cloves garlic, minced
- 1/3 cup olive oil

- 3 tablespoons cider vinegar
- 1 teaspoon dried oregano
- 1/2 teaspoon salt
- 1/2 teaspoon ground black pepper
- 4 avocados - peeled, pitted and diced

DIRECTIONS

1. In a large bowl, mix corn, olives, red bell pepper and onion.
2. In a small bowl, mix garlic, olive oil, lemon juice, cider vinegar, oregano, salt and pepper. Pour into the corn mixture and toss to coat. Cover and chill in the refrigerator 8 hours, or overnight.
3. Stir avocados into the mixture before serving.

SPANAKOPITA
Servings: 27 | Prep: 30m | Cooks: 1h5m | Total: 1h35m

NUTRITION FACTS

Calories: 246 | Carbohydrates: 15.9g | Fat: 18.4g | Protein: 5g | Cholesterol: 62mg

INGREDIENTS

- 1/2 cup vegetable oil
- 2 large onions, chopped
- 2 tablespoons chopped fresh dill
- 2 (10 ounce) packages frozen chopped spinach - thawed, drained and squeezed dry
- 2 tablespoons all-purpose flour

- 2 (4 ounce) packages feta cheese, crumbled
- 4 eggs, lightly beaten
- salt and pepper to taste
- 1 1/2 (16 ounce) packages phyllo dough
- 3/4 pound butter, melted

DIRECTIONS

1. Preheat oven to 350 degrees F (175 degrees C).
2. Heat vegetable oil in a large saucepan over medium heat. Slowly cook and stir onions until softened. Mix in spinach, dill and flour. Cook approximately 10 minutes, or until most of the moisture has been absorbed. Remove from heat. Mix in feta cheese, eggs, salt and pepper.
3. Separate one sheet of phyllo from the stack and evenly brush with a light coating of butter. Place another sheet of phyllo over the butter and press the two sheets together. Cut the layered phyllo dough into long strips about 3 inches wide. Keep the remaining phyllo covered with plastic wrap to keep it from drying out.

4. Lay out one strip of phyllo at a time on your work surface with one of the narrow ends close to you. Place a heaping tablespoon of filling 1 inch from the end closest to you. Fold the bottom right corner over the filling to the left edge to form a triangle. Fold the triangle up, bringing the point at the bottom left up to rest along the left edge. Turn the lower left corner over to touch the right edge. Continue turning the triangle over in this manner until you reach the end of the phyllo.
5. Repeat with the remaining filling and phyllo dough. Place filled phyllo dough triangles on a large baking sheet and brush with the remaining butter. (At this point, the pastries may be frozen. See Cook's Note.)
6. Bake in the preheated oven until the phyllo is golden brown, 45 minutes to 1 hour.

TEXAS CAVIAR
Servings: 16 | Prep: 15m | Cooks: 1h | Total: 1h15m

NUTRITION FACTS

Calories: 107 | Carbohydrates: 11.8g | Fat: 5.4g | Protein: 3.5g | Cholesterol: 0mg

INGREDIENTS

- 1/2 onion, chopped
- 1 green bell pepper, chopped
- 1 bunch green onions, chopped
- 2 jalapeno peppers, chopped
- 1 tablespoon minced garlic
- 1 pint cherry tomatoes, quartered
- 1 (8 ounce) bottle zesty Italian dressing
- 1 (15 ounce) can black beans, drained
- 1 (15 ounce) can black-eyed peas, drained
- 1/2 teaspoon ground coriander
- 1 bunch chopped fresh cilantro

DIRECTIONS

1. In a large bowl, mix together onion, green bell pepper, green onions, jalapeno peppers, garlic, cherry tomatoes, zesty Italian dressing, black beans, black-eyed peas and coriander. Cover and chill in the refrigerator approximately 2 hours. Toss with desired amount of fresh cilantro to serve.

FRESH SALSA
Servings: 48 | Prep: 20m | Cooks: 15m | Total: 35m

NUTRITION FACTS

Calories: 6 | Carbohydrates: 1.5g | Fat: 0g | Protein: 0.2g | Cholesterol: 0mg

INGREDIENTS

- 4 jalapeno chile peppers
- 5 cloves garlic, finely chopped
- 1 onion, finely chopped
- 1 tablespoon white sugar

- 1 teaspoon salt
- 1/4 teaspoon ground cumin
- 1 (10 ounce) can diced tomatoes with green chile peppers
- 1 (28 ounce) can whole peeled tomatoes

DIRECTIONS

1. Preheat oven to 400 degrees F (200 degrees C).
2. Place jalapeno chile peppers on a medium baking sheet. Bake in the preheated oven 15 minutes, or until roasted. Remove from heat and chop off stems.
3. Place jalapeno chile peppers, garlic, onion, white sugar, salt, ground cumin and diced tomatoes with green chile peppers in a blender or food processor. Chop using the pulse setting for a few seconds. Mix in whole peeled tomatoes. Chop using the pulse setting to attain desired consistency. Transfer to a medium bowl. Cover and chill in the refrigerator until serving.

BACON AND DATE APPETIZER
Servings: 6 | Prep: 30m | Cooks: 5m | Total: 35m

NUTRITION FACTS

Calories: 560 | Carbohydrates: 32.2g | Fat: 43.7g | Protein: 13.7g | Cholesterol: 51mg

INGREDIENTS

- 1 (8 ounce) package pitted dates
- 4 ounces almonds

- 1 pound sliced bacon

DIRECTIONS

1. Preheat the broiler.
2. Slit dates. Place one almond inside each date. Wrap dates with bacon, using toothpicks to hold them together.
3. Broil 10 minutes, or until bacon is evenly brown and crisp.

GARLIC-GINGER CHICKEN WINGS
Servings: 10 | Prep: 10m | Cooks: 1h | Total: 1h15m | Additional: 5m

NUTRITION FACTS

Calories: 230 | Carbohydrates: 21.1g | Fat: 7.5g | Protein: 18.8g | Cholesterol: 48mg

INGREDIENTS

- cooking spray
- 5 pounds chicken wings, separated at joints, tips discarded
- salt and ground black pepper to taste
- 3 tablespoons hot sauce (such as Frank's Red Hot ®)
- 2 tablespoons vegetable oil
- 1 cup all-purpose flour

- 3 crushed garlic cloves
- 2 tablespoons minced fresh ginger root
- 1 tablespoon Asian chile pepper sauce
- 1/2 cup rice vinegar
- 1/2 cup packed brown sugar
- 1 tablespoon soy sauce

DIRECTIONS

1. Preheat oven to 400 degrees F (200 degrees C). Line 2 baking sheets with aluminum foil; grease the foil with cooking spray.
2. Place the chicken in a large mixing bowl. Season with salt, pepper, and hot sauce. Add the vegetable oil; toss to coat.
3. Place the flour and wings in a large, food-safe plastic bag. Hold the bag closed tightly, and shake to coat the wings entirely with the flour; no wet spots should remain. Arrange the wings on the prepared baking sheets, making sure none of the pieces are touching one another. Spray wings with additional cooking spray.
4. Bake in the preheated oven for 30 minutes, turn all the wings, and return to the oven to cook until crispy and no longer pink in the center, about 30 minutes more.
5. Whisk together the garlic, ginger, chili paste, rice vinegar, brown sugar, and soy sauce in a saucepan. Bring the mixture to a boil and immediately remove from heat.
6. Put about half the wings in a large mixing bowl. Pour about half the sauce over the wings. Toss the wings with tongs to coat evenly; transfer to a tray and allow to sit about 5 minutes to allow the sauce to soak into the wings before serving. Repeat with remaining wings and sauce.

HOT CRAB DIP
Servings: 40 | Prep: 10m | Cooks: 30m | Total: 40m

NUTRITION FACTS

Calories: 81 | Carbohydrates: 0.6g | Fat: 7g | Protein: 4g | Cholesterol: 26mg

INGREDIENTS

- 2 (8 ounce) packages cream cheese, softened

- 1 1/2 tablespoons fresh lemon juice

- 4 tablespoons mayonnaise
- 2 cups shredded Cheddar cheese
- 2 (6 ounce) cans crabmeat
- 2 teaspoons hot sauce
- 2 tablespoons Worcestershire sauce
- paprika, for garnish

DIRECTIONS

1. Preheat oven to 350 degrees F (175 degrees C).
2. In a medium bowl, mix the cream cheese, mayonnaise, Cheddar cheese, crabmeat, lemon juice, hot sauce and Worcestershire sauce. Transfer to a shallow 9x13 inch baking dish. Garnish with paprika.
3. Bake in the preheated oven 30 minutes, or until golden brown and bubbly.

PARMESAN SPINACH BALLS
Servings: 10 | Prep: 15m | Cooks: 15m | Total: 30m

NUTRITION FACTS

Calories: 258 | Carbohydrates: 19.1g | Fat: 15.6g | Protein: 11.8g | Cholesterol: 108mg

INGREDIENTS

- 2 (10 ounce) packages frozen chopped spinach, thawed and drained
- 2 cups Italian-style seasoned bread crumbs
- 4 small green onion, finely chopped
- salt and pepper to taste
- 1 cup grated Parmesan cheese
- 1/2 cup butter, melted
- 4 eggs, lightly beaten

DIRECTIONS

1. Preheat oven to 350 degrees F (175 degrees C).
2. In a medium bowl, mix the frozen chopped spinach, Italian-style seasoned bread crumbs, Parmesan cheese, butter, green onion, eggs, salt and pepper. Shape the mixture into 1 inch balls.
3. Arrange the balls in a single layer on a large baking sheet. Bake in the preheated oven 10 to 15 minutes, until lightly browned.

DILL DIP
Servings: 32 | Prep: 5m | Cooks: 8h | Total: 8h5m

NUTRITION FACTS

Calories: 131 | Carbohydrates: 1.5g | Fat: 14g | Protein: 0.7g | Cholesterol: 12mg

INGREDIENTS

- 2 cups mayonnaise
- 2 cups sour cream
- 1 tablespoon dried parsley
- 3 tablespoons grated onion
- 3 tablespoons dried dill weed
- 1 1/2 tablespoons seasoning salt

DIRECTIONS

1. In a medium bowl combine the mayonnaise, sour cream, parsley, onion, dill weed, and salt. Mix all together, cover, and refrigerate overnight.

QUICK ASIAN LETTUCE WRAPS
Servings: 4 | Prep: 15m | Cooks: 32m | Total: 47m

NUTRITION FACTS

Calories: 836 | Carbohydrates: 95.5g | Fat: 31g | Protein: 45.8g | Cholesterol: 74mg

INGREDIENTS

- 4 cups water
- 2 cups uncooked white rice
- 1 tablespoon vegetable oil
- 1 pound ground pork
- 1 bunch green onions, thinly sliced
- 1/2 teaspoon minced garlic
- 1 (14 ounce) package firm tofu, drained and cubed
- 2 carrots, shredded
- 3 tablespoons hoisin sauce
- 2 tablespoons soy sauce
- 1 teaspoon sesame oil
- 1/4 teaspoon hot chile paste
- 11 head iceberg lettuce leaves, separated

DIRECTIONS

1. In a saucepan combine the water and rice. Bring to a boil, cover, and reduce heat to a simmer. Simmer for 20 minutes, until water is absorbed. Set aside and keep warm.
2. Heat oil in a wok over medium-high heat. Cook the pork, green onions, and garlic for 5 to 7 minutes, or until lightly brown. Add the tofu, carrot, Hoisin, and soy sauce, stirring frequently until heated through. Remove from heat, and stir in the sesame oil and chile paste.
3. To serve: spoon a small amount of rice into each lettuce leaf, top with the stir-fry mixture, and drizzle with additional soy sauce or hoisin, if desired. Wrap the lettuce leaf to enclose the filling.

CARAMEL SNACK MIX

Servings: 30 | Prep: 10m | Cooks: 1h | Total: 1h10m

NUTRITION FACTS

Calories: 262 | Carbohydrates: 36.9g | Fat: 12.6g | Protein: 3.4g | Cholesterol: 12mg

INGREDIENTS

- 1/2 cup butter
- 3/4 cup white corn syrup
- 1 cup packed brown sugar
- 1 cup chopped pecans
- 1 cup almonds
- 1 (12 ounce) package crispy corn and rice cereal

DIRECTIONS

1. Preheat oven to 275 degrees F (135 degrees C). Spray a large roasting pan with non-stick cooking spray.
2. In a medium-size microwave safe bowl, mix butter, white corn syrup and brown sugar. Place the mixture in the microwave and cook 2 minutes, or until butter melts.
3. Place the cereal, pecans and almonds into the prepared roasting pan. Pour the melted butter mixture over the cereal and nuts and mix gently until the cereal and nuts are coated.
4. Bake for 1 hour, stirring every 15 minutes.
5. As the snack mix is cooling, be sure to continue to stir so that the mix will not harden in one big lump.

SWEET AND SOUR MEATBALLS

Servings: 12 | Prep: 20m | Cooks: 1h30m | Total: 1h50m

NUTRITION FACTS

Calories: 152 | Carbohydrates: 17.4g | Fat: 5.6g | Protein: 8.3g | Cholesterol: 38mg

INGREDIENTS

- 1 (12 fluid ounce) can or bottle chile sauce
- 2 teaspoons lemon juice
- 9 ounces grape jelly
- 1 pound lean ground beef
- 1 egg, beaten
- 1 large onion, grated
- salt to taste

DIRECTIONS

1. Whisk together the chili sauce, lemon juice and grape jelly. Pour into slow cooker and simmer over low heat until warm.
2. Combine ground beef, egg, onion and salt. Mix well and form into 1 inch balls. Add to sauce and simmer for 1 1/2 hours.

SPICY TORTILLA ROLL-UPS

Servings: 30 | Prep: 1h10 | Cooks: 5m | Total: 1h15m

NUTRITION FACTS

Calories: 109 | Carbohydrates: 14.2g | Fat: 2.8g | Protein: 2.8g | Cholesterol: 8mg

INGREDIENTS

- 1 (8 ounce) package cream cheese, softened
- 1 (2 ounce) can chopped black olives
- 1 (4 ounce) can diced green chiles
- 1 (4 ounce) jar sliced pimento peppers, drained
- 2 green onions, minced
- 3 tablespoons hot pepper sauce
- 3 tablespoons chopped fresh cilantro
- 10 (10 inch) flour tortillas

DIRECTIONS

1. In a medium-size mixing bowl, combine cream cheese, olives, chiles, pimentos, green onions, hot sauce and fresh cilantro. Spread the mixture onto tortillas. Roll the tortillas up and refrigerate for at least 1 hour.
2. Slice the roll ups and serve.

SWEET AND SOUR SAUCE

Servings: 48 | Prep: 5m | Cooks: 15m | Total: 20m

NUTRITION FACTS

Calories: 32 | Carbohydrates: 8.1g | Fat: 0g | Protein: 0.2g | Cholesterol: 0mg

INGREDIENTS

- 2 cups water
- 2/3 cup distilled white vinegar
- 1 1/2 cups white sugar
- 1 (6 ounce) can tomato paste
- 1 (8 ounce) can pineapple tidbits, drained
- 3 tablespoons cornstarch

DIRECTIONS

1. In a medium saucepan over medium heat, mix together water, distilled white vinegar, white sugar, tomato paste, pineapple tidbits and cornstarch. Cook, stirring occasionally, 15 minutes, or until mixture reaches desired color and consistency.

SAUSAGE STUFFED MUSHROOMS

Servings: 10 | Prep: 20m | Cooks: 3m | Total: 23m

NUTRITION FACTS

Calories: 178 | Carbohydrates: 1.6g | Fat: 17g | Protein: 5g | Cholesterol: 40mg

INGREDIENTS

- 1/2 pound ground pork sausage
- 1 (8 ounce) package cream cheese, softened
- 1 (8 ounce) package fresh mushrooms, stems removed

DIRECTIONS

1. Preheat the broiler.
2. Place sausage in a large, deep skillet. Cook over medium high heat until evenly brown. Drain and transfer to a medium bowl.
3. Blend cream cheese with the sausage. Stuff mushroom caps with the cream cheese and sausage mixture.
4. Arrange stuffed mushroom caps on a medium baking sheet. Broil in the preheated oven 2 to 3 minutes, until lightly browned.

SPICED PECANS

Servings: 6 | Prep: 10m | Cooks: 30m | Total: 40m

NUTRITION FACTS

Calories: 443 | Carbohydrates: 24.7g | Fat: 39g | Protein: 5.6g | Cholesterol: 0mg

INGREDIENTS

- 1 egg white, lightly beaten
- 1 tablespoon water
- 3 cups pecan halves
- 1/2 cup white sugar
- 1/2 teaspoon salt
- 1 teaspoon ground cinnamon
- 1/2 teaspoon ground cloves
- 1/2 teaspoon ground nutmeg

DIRECTIONS

1. Preheat oven to 350 degrees F (175 degrees C). Line a baking sheet with aluminum foil.
2. In a small bowl beat the egg white with the water. Stir in the pecans, mixing until well moistened.

3. In a small bowl, mix together sugar, salt, cinnamon, cloves and nutmeg. Sprinkle over the moistened nuts. Spread nuts on prepared pan.
4. Bake in preheated oven for 30 minutes, stirring once or twice. Be careful not to overcook and burn the nuts.

HOT CORN DIP

Servings: 45 | Prep: 15m | Cooks: 30m | Total: 45m

NUTRITION FACTS

Calories: 29 | Carbohydrates: 3.3g | Fat: 1.7g | Protein: 0.8g | Cholesterol: 5mg

INGREDIENTS

- 1 (15 ounce) can white corn, drained
- 2 eggs
- 1 (15 ounce) can yellow corn, drained
- 1 (10 ounce) can diced tomatoes with green chile peppers, drained
- 1/2 teaspoon garlic powder
- chopped fresh cilantro to taste
- 1 (8 ounce) package cream cheese, diced and softened
- 1/2 teaspoon chili powder

DIRECTIONS

1. Preheat oven to 350 degrees F (175 degrees C).
2. In a medium baking dish, mix white corn, yellow corn, diced tomatoes with green chile peppers, cream cheese, chili powder, garlic powder and cilantro.
3. Bake in the preheated oven 30 minutes, or until hot bubbly .

CAJUN APPETIZER MEATBALLS

Servings: 5 | Prep: 15m | Cooks: 40m | Total: 1h

NUTRITION FACTS

Calories: 504| Carbohydrates: 45g | Fat: 25.4g | Protein: 22.9g | Cholesterol: 133mg

INGREDIENTS

- 1 pound lean ground beef
- 1 1/2 teaspoons hot pepper sauce
- 2 tablespoons Cajun seasoning
- 1 tablespoon Worcestershire sauce
- 1 tablespoon dried parsley
- 1/4 cup finely chopped onion
- 1/4 cup fresh bread crumbs
- 1/4 cup milk
- 1 egg
- 1/2 cup barbeque sauce

- 1/2 cup peach preserves

DIRECTIONS

1. Preheat oven to 350 degrees F (175 degrees C). Lightly grease a medium baking sheet.
2. In a large bowl, mix thoroughly the ground beef, hot pepper sauce, Cajun seasoning, Worcestershire sauce, parsley, onion, bread crumbs, milk, and egg.
3. Form the mixture into golf ball sized meatballs and place on the prepared baking sheet. Bake in preheated oven for 30 to 40 minutes, or until there is no pink left in the middle.
4. In a small bowl, combine the barbeque sauce and peach preserves.
5. When meatballs are done, place in a serving dish and cover with the barbeque sauce mixture. Toss to coat.

FRESH SALSA
Servings: 48 | Prep: 20m | Cooks: 15m | Total: 30m

NUTRITION FACTS

Calories: 6 | Carbohydrates: 1.5g | Fat: 0g | Protein: 0.2g | Cholesterol: 0mg

INGREDIENTS

- 4 jalapeno chile peppers
- 5 cloves garlic, finely chopped
- 1 onion, finely chopped
- 1 tablespoon white sugar

- 1 teaspoon salt
- 1/4 teaspoon ground cumin
- 1 (10 ounce) can diced tomatoes with green chile peppers
- 1 (28 ounce) can whole peeled tomatoes

DIRECTIONS

1. Preheat oven to 400 degrees F (200 degrees C).
2. Place jalapeno chile peppers on a medium baking sheet. Bake in the preheated oven 15 minutes, or until roasted. Remove from heat and chop off stems.
3. Place jalapeno chile peppers, garlic, onion, white sugar, salt, ground cumin and diced tomatoes with green chile peppers in a blender or food processor. Chop using the pulse setting for a few seconds. Mix in whole peeled tomatoes. Chop using the pulse setting to attain desired consistency. Transfer to a medium bowl. Cover and chill in the refrigerator until serving.

BACON AND DATE APPETIZER

Servings: 6 | Prep: 30m | Cooks: 5m | Total: 35m

NUTRITION FACTS

Calories: 560 | Carbohydrates: 32.2g | Fat: 43.7g | Protein: 13.7g | Cholesterol: 51mg

INGREDIENTS

- 1 (8 ounce) package pitted dates
- 4 ounces almonds
- 1 pound sliced bacon

DIRECTIONS

1. Preheat the broiler.
2. Slit dates. Place one almond inside each date. Wrap dates with bacon, using toothpicks to hold them together.
3. Broil 10 minutes, or until bacon is evenly brown and crisp.

GARLIC-GINGER CHICKEN WINGS

Servings: 10 | Prep: 10m | Cooks: 1h | Total: 1h15m | Additional: 5m

NUTRITION FACTS

Calories: 230 | Carbohydrates: 21.1g | Fat: 7.5g | Protein: 18.8g | Cholesterol: 48mg

INGREDIENTS

- cooking spray
- 5 pounds chicken wings, separated at joints, tips discarded
- salt and ground black pepper to taste
- 3 tablespoons hot sauce (such as Frank's Red Hot ®)
- 2 tablespoons vegetable oil
- 1 cup all-purpose flour
- 3 crushed garlic cloves
- 2 tablespoons minced fresh ginger root
- 1 tablespoon Asian chile pepper sauce
- 1/2 cup rice vinegar
- 1/2 cup packed brown sugar
- 1 tablespoon soy sauce

DIRECTIONS

1. Preheat oven to 400 degrees F (200 degrees C). Line 2 baking sheets with aluminum foil; grease the foil with cooking spray.

2. Place the chicken in a large mixing bowl. Season with salt, pepper, and hot sauce. Add the vegetable oil; toss to coat.

3. Place the flour and wings in a large, food-safe plastic bag. Hold the bag closed tightly, and shake to coat the wings entirely with the flour; no wet spots should remain. Arrange the wings on the prepared baking sheets, making sure none of the pieces are touching one another. Spray wings with additional cooking spray.

4. Bake in the preheated oven for 30 minutes, turn all the wings, and return to the oven to cook until crispy and no longer pink in the center, about 30 minutes more.

5. Whisk together the garlic, ginger, chili paste, rice vinegar, brown sugar, and soy sauce in a saucepan. Bring the mixture to a boil and immediately remove from heat.

6. Put about half the wings in a large mixing bowl. Pour about half the sauce over the wings. Toss the wings with tongs to coat evenly; transfer to a tray and allow to sit about 5 minutes to allow the sauce to soak into the wings before serving. Repeat with remaining wings and sauce.

POT STICKERS TRADITIONAL
Servings: 15 | Prep: 1h | Cooks: 10m | Total: 7h10m | Additional: 6h

NUTRITION FACTS

Calories: 166 | Carbohydrates: 17.3g | Fat: 8.2g | Protein: 5.7g | Cholesterol: 12mg

INGREDIENTS

- 1/2 pound ground pork
- 1/2 medium head cabbage, finely chopped
- 1 green onion, finely chopped
- 2 slices fresh ginger root, finely chopped
- 2 water chestnuts, drained and finely chopped
- 1 teaspoon salt
- 1/2 teaspoon white sugar

- 1 teaspoon sesame oil
- 1 (14 ounce) package wonton wrappers
- 5 tablespoons vegetable oil
- 3/4 cup water
- 1 tablespoon chili oil
- 1 tablespoon soy sauce
- 1 teaspoon rice vinegar

DIRECTIONS

1. Crumble pork into a large, deep skillet. Cook over medium high heat until evenly brown. Drain and set aside.

2. In a medium bowl, mix together the pork, cabbage, green onion, ginger, water chestnuts, salt, sugar and sesame oil. Chill in the refrigerator 6 to 8 hours, or overnight.

3. Place a tablespoon of the pork mixture into each of the wonton wrappers. Fold the wrappers, and seal the edges with a moistened fork.

4. In a large, deep skillet, heat 3 tablespoons vegetable oil over medium high heat. Place the pot stickers into the oil seam sides up. Heat 30 seconds to a minute. Pour water into the skillet. Gently boil 7 to 8 minutes, until oil and water begins to sizzle, then add remaining oil. When the bottoms begin to brown, remove pot stickers from heat.

5. In a small serving bowl, mix together the chili oil, soy sauce, and vinegar, adjusting proportions to taste.

BAKED MARYLAND LUMP CRAB CAKES
Servings: 12 | Prep: 15 | Cooks: 25m | Total: 40m

NUTRITION FACTS

Calories: 92 | Carbohydrates: 2.5g | Fat: 4.1g | Protein: 10.8g | Cholesterol: 34mg

INGREDIENTS

- 1/4 cup bread crumbs
- 1/4 cup bread crumbs
- 1 teaspoon dried parsley
- 1 teaspoon mustard powder
- 3/4 cup cholesterol-free egg product
- 1/8 teaspoon black pepper

- 2 teaspoons seafood seasoning, such as Old Bay
- 1 tablespoon mayonnaise
- 2 tablespoons butter, melted
- 1 teaspoon Worcestershire sauce
- 1 pound lump crab meat

1. **DIRECTIONS**
2. Preheat oven to 375 degrees F (190 degrees C). Grease a baking sheet.
3. Combine bread crumbs, baking powder, parsley, mustard powder, pepper, and seafood seasoning; set aside. Stir together mayonnaise, butter, Worcestershire, and egg product until smooth. Fold in crab meat, then fold in bread crumb mixture until well blended.
4. Shape mixture into 12 crab cakes, about 3/4 inch thick, and place onto prepared baking sheet.
5. Bake in preheated oven for 15 minutes, then turn the crab cakes over, and bake an additional 10 to 15 minutes, until nicely browned.

BAKED ZUCCHINI FRIES
Servings: 4 | Prep: 15m | Cooks: 20m | Total: 35m

NUTRITION FACTS

Calories: 135 | Carbohydrates: 15g | Fat: 5g | Protein: 8.6 g | Cholesterol: 97mg

INGREDIENTS

- cooking spray
- 1/2 cup bread crumbs
- 1/4 cup grated Parmesan cheese
- 2 eggs, beaten
- 3 zucchinis - ends trimmed, halved, and cut into 1/2-inch strips

DIRECTIONS

1. Preheat oven to 425 degrees F (220 degrees C). Line a baking sheet with aluminum foil and spray with cooking spray.
2. Stir bread crumbs and Parmesan cheese together in a shallow bowl. Whisk eggs in a separate shallow bowl.
3. Working in batches, dip zucchini strips into egg mixture, shake to remove any excess, and roll strips in bread crumb mixture to coat. Transfer coated zucchini strips to the prepared baking sheet.
4. ☐ Bake zucchini fries in the preheated oven, turning once, until golden and crisp, 20 to 24 minutes.

KALE CHIPS

Servings: 2 | Prep: 15m | Cooks: 35m | Total: 50m

NUTRITION FACTS

Calories: 174 | Carbohydrates: 22.5g | Fat: 8.3g | Protein: 7.4g | Cholesterol: 0mg

INGREDIENTS

- 1 bunch kale
- 1 tablespoon extra-virgin olive oil, divided
- 1 tablespoon sherry vinegar
- 1 pinch sea salt, to taste

DIRECTIONS

1. Preheat an oven to 300 degrees F (150 degrees C).
2. Cut away inner ribs from each kale leaf and discard; tear the leaves into pieces of uniform size. (I made my pieces about the size of a small potato chip.) Wash torn kale pieces and spin dry in a salad spinner or dry with paper towels until they're very dry.
3. Put the kale pieces into a large resealable bag (or use a bowl if you don't mind getting your hands oily). Add about half the olive oil; seal and squeeze the bag so the oil gets distributed evenly on the kale pieces. Add the remaining oil and squeeze the bag more, until all kale pieces are evenly coated with oil and slightly 'massaged.' Sprinkle the vinegar over the kale leaves, reseal the bag, and shake to spread the vinegar evenly over the leaves. Spread the leaves evenly onto a baking sheet.
4. Roast in the preheated oven until mostly crisp, about 35 minutes. Season with salt and serve immediately.

INSANELY AMAZING JALAPENO CHEESE DIP

Servings: 8 | Prep: 10m | Cooks: 30m | Total: 40m

NUTRITION FACTS

Calories: 438 | Carbohydrates: 34.7g | Fat: 28.1g | Protein: 12.7g | Cholesterol: 25mg

INGREDIENTS

- 1 (4 ounce) can diced jalapeno peppers
- 1 cup shredded Parmesan cheese
- 1/2 cup shredded Cheddar cheese
- 1 cup mayonnaise
- 1 (4 ounce) can chopped green chilies
- 1 round loaf sourdough bread

DIRECTIONS

1. Preheat an oven to 350 degrees F (175 degrees C).
2. Combine jalapeno peppers, Parmesan cheese, Cheddar cheese, mayonnaise, and green chilies in a bowl. Cut the top off of the sourdough bread and hollow out the center to create a bowl. Fill the bread bowl with the jalapeno mixture.
3. Bake in the preheated oven for 30 minutes.

PARMESAN GARLIC BREAD

Servings: 15 | Prep: 12m | Cooks: 12m | Total: 27m

NUTRITION FACTS

Calories: 267 | Carbohydrates: 31.8g | Fat: 12.7g | Protein: 7g | Cholesterol: 31mg

INGREDIENTS

- 1/2 cup butter, melted
- 1 teaspoon garlic salt
- 1/4 teaspoon dried rosemary
- 1/8 teaspoon dried basil
- 1/8 teaspoon garlic powder
- 1 tablespoon grated Parmesan cheese
- 1 (1 pound) loaf French bread, halved lengthwise
- 1/8 teaspoon dried thyme

DIRECTIONS

1. Preheat oven to 300 degrees F (150 degrees C).
2. In a small bowl, mix butter, garlic salt, rosemary, basil, thyme, garlic powder and Parmesan cheese.
3. Spread each half of the French bread with equal portions of the butter mixture. Sprinkle with additional Parmesan cheese, if desired.

4. Place bread halves, crusts down, on a medium baking sheet. Bake in the preheated oven 10 to 12 minutes, or until the edges are very lightly browned.

AWESOME EGG ROLLS
Servings: 8 | Prep: 30m | Cooks: 15m | Total: 45m

NUTRITION FACTS

Calories: 208 | Carbohydrates: 17.7g | Fat: 12.3g | Protein: 7.2g | Cholesterol: 49mg

INGREDIENTS

- 6 cups cabbage, shredded
- 1 carrot, shredded
- 1/2 cup fresh bean sprouts
- 1 celery stalk, diced
- black pepper to taste
- cornstarch
- vegetable oil for frying
- 2 tablespoons chopped onion (optional)
- 1 (4 ounce) can shrimp, drained
- 2 tablespoons soy sauce
- 1/8 teaspoon garlic powder
- 1 egg, beaten
- 20 egg roll wrappers

DIRECTIONS

1. In a large bowl, mix together cabbage, carrots, sprouts, celery, and onion. Stir in shrimp, soy sauce, garlic powder, and black pepper.
2. Pour beaten egg into a skillet placed over medium heat; cook flat and thin, flipping once, until done. Remove from skillet, cool, and chop finely. Stir egg into cabbage mixture. Sprinkle top with cornstarch, mix, and allow to sit 10 minutes.
3. Mix 1 tablespoon cornstarch with 2 tablespoons cold water. Set aside.
4. Place 2 or 3 tablespoons of the shrimp mixture into the center of an egg roll skin. Dip a spoon into the water and cornstarch mixture, and moisten all corners but the bottom corner. Fold the egg roll skin from the bottom over the mixture, making a tight tube of the shrimp mixture. Fold corners in from the sides, and press to stick against folded roll. Then roll the rest of the way. Repeat with remaining egg roll wrappers.
5. Pour vegetable oil into a deep frying pan to a depth of 3 or 4 inches, and heat oil to 350 degrees F (175 degrees C). Carefully place egg rolls into hot oil, and fry until golden brown. Remove to paper towels.

EASY SAUSAGE CHEESE BALLS
Servings: 36 | Prep: 10m | Cooks: 15m | Total: 25m

NUTRITION FACTS

Calories: 137 | Carbohydrates: 7.5g | Fat: 9.4g | Protein: 5.5g | Cholesterol: 22mg

INGREDIENTS

- 1 pound sausage

- 4 cups shredded Cheddar cheese

- 3 cups baking mix

DIRECTIONS

1. Preheat oven to 400 degrees F (200 degrees C).
2. In a medium bowl, combine the sausage, cheese, and dry baking mix. Mix together, and shape mixture into walnut-sized balls. Place on a foil-lined cookie sheet.
3. Bake for 12 to 15 minutes. Serve hot.

ARTICHOKE DIP

Servings: 10 | Prep: 1h | Cooks: 1h | Total: 2h

NUTRITION FACTS

Calories: 79 | Carbohydrates: 1.1g | Fat: 1.1g | Protein: 2.4g | Cholesterol: 8mg

INGREDIENTS

- 1 cup mayonnaise

- 1 cup grated Parmesan cheese

- 2 (6.5 ounce) jars marinated artichoke hearts, drained

- 2 cups shredded mozzarella cheese

- 1 1/2 teaspoons garlic powder

- 1 teaspoon paprika

DIRECTIONS

1. Preheat oven to 350 degrees F (175 degrees C).
2. In a large bowl, thoroughly mix the mayonnaise, Parmesan, artichoke, mozzarella and garlic powder. Transfer the mixture to an 8x8 inch baking dish.
3. Bake 30 minutes, or until the surface is lightly browned and bubbly.
4. Sprinkle with paprika and serve warm

SALSA

Servings: 96 | Prep: 30m | Cooks: 20m | Total: 50m

NUTRITION FACTS

Calories: 9 | Carbohydrates: 2g | Fat: 0.1g | Protein: 4g | Cholesterol: 0mg

INGREDIENTS

- 6 pounds roma (plum) tomatoes
- 1/4 pound roma (plum) tomatoes, chopped
- 2 tablespoons garlic powder
- 1/3 bunch fresh cilantro, chopped
- 1 red onion, chopped
- 1 yellow onion, chopped

- 1/4 cup lemon juice
- 1 1/2 tablespoons salt
- 1 tablespoon ground cayenne pepper
- 1 1/2 teaspoons ground cumin
- 1 white onion, chopped
- 1 pound jalapeno peppers, chopped

DIRECTIONS

1. Bring a large saucepan of water to boil. Briefly place 6 pounds tomatoes into water to loosen skins and set color. Drain, peel and crush.
2. Mix chopped tomatoes, garlic powder, lemon juice, salt, cayenne pepper and cumin into the saucepan with crushed tomatoes. Whip to desired thickness. Bring to a boil. Mix in red onion, white onion, yellow onion, jalapeno peppers and cilantro. Continue boiling until vegetables are soft and mixture has reached desired consistency. Remove from heat. Refrigerate until serving.

BREAD MACHINE GARLIC BREAD
Servings: 12 | Prep: 10m | Cooks: 30m | Total: 3h10m

NUTRITION FACTS

Calories: 142 | Carbohydrates: 26.9g | Fat: 1.6g | Protein: 4.7g | Cholesterol: 3mg

INGREDIENTS

- 1 cup warm water (110 degrees F)
- 1 tablespoon butter
- 1 tablespoon dry milk powder
- 1 tablespoon white sugar
- 2 teaspoons active dry yeast

- 1 1/2 teaspoons salt
- 1 1/2 tablespoons dried parsley
- 2 teaspoons garlic powder
- 3 cups bread flour

DIRECTIONS

1. Place ingredients in the pan of the bread machine in the order recommended by the manufacturer. Select Basic Bread cycle; press Start.

BAKED BUFFALO CHICKEN DIP

Servings: 8 | Prep: 15m | Cooks: 30m | Total: 30m

NUTRITION FACTS

Calories: 407 | Carbohydrates: 3.2g | Fat: 35.9g | Protein: 17.1g | Cholesterol: 107mg

INGREDIENTS

- 3 cups diced cooked rotisserie chicken
- 2 (8 ounce) packages cream cheese, softened
- 3/4 cup hot pepper sauce (such as Frank's RedHot®)
- 1/2 cup shredded pepper Jack cheese
- 1/2 cup blue cheese dressing

- 1/2 cup crumbled blue cheese
- 1/2 teaspoon seafood seasoning (such as Old Bay®)
- 1 pinch cayenne pepper, or to taste
- 2 tablespoons shredded pepper Jack cheese
- 1 pinch cayenne pepper, for garnish

DIRECTIONS

1. Preheat oven to 400 degrees F (200 degrees C).
2. Combine chicken, cream cheese, hot pepper sauce, 1/2 cup pepper Jack cheese, blue cheese dressing, crumbled blue cheese, seafood seasoning, and cayenne pepper in a large bowl.
3. Transfer chicken mixture to a 9-inch round baking dish and sprinkle with 2 tablespoons pepper Jack cheese.
4. Bake until lightly browned, 15 to 20 minutes. Remove from oven and garnish with cayenne pepper.

HOT ONION DIP

Servings: 6 | Prep: 15m | Cooks: 12h | Total: 12h15m

NUTRITION FACTS

Calories: 84 | Carbohydrates: 0.8g | Fat: 7.9g | Protein: 2.7g | Cholesterol: 20mg

INGREDIENTS

- 3 (8 ounce) packages cream cheese, softened
- 1 onion, finely chopped

- 1/2 cup mayonnaise
- 2 cups grated Parmesan cheese

DIRECTIONS

1. Preheat oven to 400 degrees F (200 degrees C). Lightly grease a medium baking dish.
2. In the prepared dish, mix the cream cheese, onion, Parmesan cheese and mayonnaise.
3. Bake in the preheated oven 30 minutes, or until bubbly and lightly browned.

WARM BLUE CHEESE DIP WITH GARLIC AND BACON
Servings: 14 | Prep: 30m | Cooks: 30m | Total: 1h

NUTRITION FACTS

Calories: 155 | Carbohydrates: 1.1g | Fat: 14.7g | Protein: 4.7g | Cholesterol: 35mg

INGREDIENTS

- 7 slices bacon
- 2 cloves garlic, peeled and minced
- 1 (8 ounce) package cream cheese, softened
- 1/4 cup half-and-half
- 4 ounces blue cheese, crumbled
- 2 tablespoons chopped fresh chives

DIRECTIONS

1. Place bacon in a large, deep skillet. Cook over medium high heat until evenly brown. Remove bacon from skillet, drain on paper towels and crumble.
2. Place garlic in hot bacon grease. Cook and stir until soft, about 1 minute. Remove from heat.
3. Preheat oven to 350 degrees F (175 degrees C). Place cream cheese and half-and-half in a medium bowl. Beat with an electric mixer until blended. Stir in bacon, garlic, blue cheese and chives. Transfer mixture to a medium baking dish.
4. Bake covered in the preheated oven 30 minutes, or until lightly browned.

GRILLED BUFFALO WINGS
Servings: 8 | Prep: 15m | Cooks: 50m | Total: 1h5m

NUTRITION FACTS

Calories: 129 | Carbohydrates: 5.5g | Fat: 7.3g | Protein: 10g | Cholesterol: 30mg

INGREDIENTS

- 3 pounds chicken wings, separated at joints, tips discarded
- 1 cup Louisiana-style hot sauce
- 1 (12 fluid ounce) can or bottle cola-flavored carbonated beverage
- 1/4 teaspoon cayenne pepper, or to taste
- 1/4 teaspoon ground black pepper, or to taste
- 1 tablespoon soy sauce

DIRECTIONS

1. Preheat a grill to medium heat.
2. In a large pot, mix together the hot sauce, cola, cayenne pepper, black pepper and soy sauce. Add the wings to the sauce - frozen is okay. Place the pot to one side of the grill, so the sauce comes to a simmer.
3. Use tongs to fish wings out of the sauce, and place them on the grill for 8 to 10 minutes. Then return to the sauce to simmer. Repeat this process for about 50 minutes. The sauce will thicken. When the chicken is tender and pulls easily off of the bone, you have two options. You can dip one last time and serve for sloppy style wings, or serve right off the grill for dryer wings.

BUFFALO CAULIFLOWER
Servings: 4 | Prep: 15m | Cooks: 30m | Total: 55m

NUTRITION FACTS

Calories: 330 | Carbohydrates: 29.1g | Fat: 22.6g | Protein: 3.3g | Cholesterol: 0mg

INGREDIENTS

- olive oil cooking spray
- 3/4 cup gluten-free baking flour (such as Premium Gold® Flax and Ancient Grains All-Purpose Flour)
- 1 cup water
- 1/2 teaspoon garlic powder, or to taste
- 1 teaspoon honey

- salt and ground black pepper to taste
- 2 heads cauliflower, cut into bite-size pieces
- 2 tablespoons butter
- 1/2 cup hot pepper sauce (such as Frank's RedHot®)

DIRECTIONS

1. Preheat oven to 450 degrees F (230 degrees C). Lightly grease a baking sheet with cooking spray.
2. Mix flour, water, garlic powder, salt, and pepper together in a bowl using a whisk until batter is smooth and somewhat runny. Add cauliflower to batter and mix until cauliflower is coated; spread onto the baking sheet.
3. Bake in the preheated oven until lightly browned, 20 to 25 minutes.
4. Melt butter in a saucepan over medium heat. Remove saucepan from heat and stir hot pepper sauce and honey into butter until smooth. Brush hot sauce mixture over each cauliflower piece, repeating brushing until all the hot sauce mixture is used.
5. Bake in the oven until cauliflower is browned, about 10 minutes. Remove baking sheet from oven and allow the cauliflower to cool 10 to 15 minutes.

LUVANN'S GUACAMOLE

Servings: 16 | Prep: 20m | Cooks: 30m | Total: 50m

NUTRITION FACTS

Calories: 46 | Carbohydrates: 3.5g | Fat: 3.7g | Protein: 0.7g | Cholesterol: 0mg

INGREDIENTS

- 2 avocados - peeled, pitted and diced
- 1 large tomato, diced
- 1/2 tablespoon chopped fresh cilantro
- 2 teaspoons salt, or to taste
- 1 onion, diced
- 2 jalapeno peppers, chopped
- 2 tablespoons fresh lime juice

DIRECTIONS

1. In a medium bowl, mash the avocados and stir in salt to taste. Mix in the tomato, onion, jalapeno, cilantro and lime juice. Cover and chill in the refrigerator at least 30 minutes before serving.

YUMMY ARTICHOKE DIP

Servings: 32 | Prep: 10m | Cooks: 25m | Total: 35m

NUTRITION FACTS

Calories: 104 | Carbohydrates: 1.1g | Fat: 10.1g | Protein: 2.4g | Cholesterol: 14mg

INGREDIENTS

- 1 (6.5 ounce) jar marinated artichoke hearts, drained and quartered
- 1 cup mayonnaise
- 1 1/2 cups grated Parmesan cheese
- 1 (8 ounce) package cream cheese, softened
- 1 (4 ounce) can chopped green chile peppers

DIRECTIONS

1. Preheat oven to 350 degrees F (175 degrees C).

2. In a medium bowl, mix the artichoke hearts, mayonnaise, 1 cup Parmesan, cream cheese and green chile peppers. Scoop the mixture into a pie pan or medium baking pan. Top with the remaining 1/2 cup of Parmesan.

3. Bake for 25 minutes or until bubbly and slightly browned. Serve warm.

CARAMELIZED CHICKEN WINGS
Servings: 6 | Prep: 5m | Cooks: 1h | Total: 1h5m

NUTRITION FACTS

Calories: 528 | Carbohydrates: 22.4g | Fat: 32.4g | Protein: 36.2g | Cholesterol: 142mg

INGREDIENTS

- 1 cup water
- 1/2 cup white sugar
- 1/3 cup soy sauce
- 2 tablespoons peanut butter
- 1 tablespoon honey
- 2 teaspoons wine vinegar
- 1 tablespoon minced garlic
- 12 large chicken wings, tips removed and wings cut in half at joint
- 1 teaspoon sesame seeds, or to taste (optional)

DIRECTIONS

1. In an electric skillet or a large skillet over medium heat, mix together the water, sugar, soy sauce, peanut butter, honey, wine vinegar, and garlic until smooth and the sugar has dissolved. Place the wings into the sauce, cover, and simmer for 30 minutes. Uncover and simmer until the wings are tender and the sauce has thickened, about 30 more minutes, spooning sauce over wings occasionally. Sprinkle with sesame seeds.

MARINATED SCALLOPS WRAPPED IN BACON
Servings: 24 | Prep: 15m | Cooks: 18m | Total: 1h33m | Additional: 1h

NUTRITION FACTS

Calories: 83 | Carbohydrates: 9.1g | Fat: 2.1g | Protein: 6.9g | Cholesterol: 17mg

INGREDIENTS

- 3/4 cup maple syrup
- 1/4 cup low sodium soy sauce
- 12 slices smoked bacon, halved
- 24 toothpicks

- 1 tablespoon Dijon mustard
- 12 large sea scallops, halved
- 2 tablespoons brown sugar

DIRECTIONS

1. Stir together maple syrup, soy sauce, and Dijon mustard in a bowl until smooth. Add the scallops, and toss to coat. Cover bowl with plastic wrap, and marinate at least one hour.
2. Preheat oven to 375 degrees F (190 degrees C). Line a rimmed baking sheet with a sheet of aluminum foil.
3. Arrange bacon pieces on baking sheet so they do not overlap. Bake in preheated oven until some of the grease has rendered out of the bacon; the bacon should still be very soft and pliable, about 8 minutes. Remove bacon from the baking sheet and pat with paper towels to remove excess grease. Drain or wipe grease from the baking sheet.
4. Wrap each scallop piece with a piece of bacon, and secure with a toothpick. Place onto baking sheet. Sprinkle the scallops with brown sugar.
5. Bake in preheated oven until the scallops are opaque and the bacon is crisp, 10 to 15 minutes, turning once.

SPICY MARYLAND CRAB DIP
Servings: 16 | Prep: 15m | Cooks: 30m | Total: 45m

NUTRITION FACTS

Calories: 111 | Carbohydrates: 1.2g | Fat: 9.2g | Protein: 5.9g | Cholesterol: 35mg

INGREDIENTS

- 1 (8 ounce) package cream cheese, softened
- 1/2 cup sour cream
- 2 tablespoons mayonnaise
- 1 1/2 tablespoons lemon juice
- 2 teaspoons Worcestershire sauce
- 1 teaspoon dry mustard
- garlic powder to taste
- 1/2 cup shredded Cheddar cheese
- 3/4 pound fresh crabmeat
- 3 dashes hot sauce
- Old Bay Seasoning TM to taste

DIRECTIONS

1. Preheat oven to 325 degrees F (165 degrees C). Lightly grease a 1 quart baking dish.

2. In a medium bowl, mix cream cheese, sour cream, mayonnaise, lemon juice, Worcestershire sauce, dry mustard, garlic powder and about 2 tablespoons of the Cheddar cheese. Fold in crabmeat, hot sauce and 2 tablespoons seafood seasoning.
3. Transfer the mixture to the prepared baking dish. Top with remaining Cheddar cheese and seafood seasoning. Bake in the preheated oven 30 minutes, or until bubbly and lightly browned.

ASPARAGUS WRAPPED IN CRISP PROSCIUTTO
Servings: 16 | Prep: 5m | Cooks: 15m | Total: 20m

NUTRITION FACTS

Calories: 64 | Carbohydrates: 0.6g | Fat: 5.4g | Protein: 3.1g | Cholesterol: 13mg

INGREDIENTS

- 1 tablespoon olive oil
- 16 spears fresh asparagus, trimmed
- 16 slices prosciutto

DIRECTIONS

1. Preheat the oven to 450 degrees F (220 degrees C). Line a baking sheet with aluminum foil, and coat with olive oil.
2. Wrap one slice of prosciutto around each asparagus spear, starting at the bottom, and spiraling up to the tip. Place the wrapped spears on the prepared baking sheet.
3. Bake for 5 minutes in the preheated oven. Remove, and shake the pan back and forth to roll the spears over. Return to the oven for another 5 minutes, or until asparagus is tender, and prosciutto is crisp. Serve immediately.

HONEY GINGER SHRIMP
Servings: 4 | Prep: 10m | Cooks: 10m | Total: 20m

NUTRITION FACTS

Calories: 166 | Carbohydrates: 4.1g | Fat: 8.1g | Protein: 19g | Cholesterol: 173mg

INGREDIENTS

- 2 tablespoons olive oil
- 1 tablespoon red pepper flakes
- 1 teaspoon honey
- 1/4 yellow onion, chopped
- 1 teaspoon ground ginger
- 1 pound medium shrimp - peeled and deveined

- 1 teaspoon chopped garlic
- salt and pepper to taste

DIRECTIONS

1. Heat the olive oil and red pepper flakes in a large skillet over medium heat. Add the onions, garlic, ginger and honey; cook and stir until fragrant. Add the shrimp, and cook for 5 minutes, stirring as needed, until shrimp are pink and opaque. Serve immediately.

MEXICAN LAYERED DIP
Servings: 10 | Prep: 10m | Cooks: 1h | Total: 2h10m

NUTRITION FACTS

Calories: 195 | Carbohydrates: 13.4g | Fat: 12.8g | Protein: 7.3g | Cholesterol: 28mg

INGREDIENTS

- 1 (16 ounce) can refried beans
- 1 (1.25 ounce) package taco seasoning mix
- 1 large tomato, seeded and chopped
- 1 cup guacamole
- 1 cup sour cream, room temperature
- 1 cup shredded sharp Cheddar cheese
- 1/2 cup chopped green onions
- 1/4 cup chopped black olives

DIRECTIONS

1. Spread refried beans in the bottom of a (1-quart) shallow edged serving dish (you can use a transparent dish if you'd like). Sprinkle the seasoning packet over the beans. Layer the diced tomatoes over the beans, the sour cream over the tomatoes, and the guacamole over the sour cream. Sprinkle the entire layered dip with cheddar cheese, followed by green onion and finishing it off with a layer of black olives. Cover and refrigerate until ready to serve.

CHERRY CHICKEN LETTUCE WRAPS
Servings: 6 | Prep: 15m | Cooks: 10m | Total: 25m

NUTRITION FACTS

Calories: 297 | Carbohydrates: 22.8g | Fat: 12.7g | Protein: 24.4g | Cholesterol: 58mg

INGREDIENTS

- 2 tablespoons canola oil, divided
- 1 1/4 pounds skinless, boneless chicken breast halves, cut into bite-size pieces
- 1 tablespoon minced fresh ginger root
- 2 tablespoons rice vinegar
- 2 tablespoons teriyaki sauce
- 1 tablespoon honey
- 2 tablespoons canola oil, divided

- 1 pound dark sweet cherries, pitted and halved
- 1 1/2 cups shredded carrots
- 1/2 cup chopped green onion
- 1/3 cup toasted and sliced almonds
- 12 lettuce leaves
- 1 pound dark sweet cherries, pitted and halved

DIRECTIONS

1. Heat 1 tablespoon oil in a large skillet over medium-high heat. Saute chicken and ginger in hot oil until chicken is cooked through, 7 to 10 minutes. Set aside.
2. Whisk vinegar, teriyaki sauce, remaining 1 tablespoon oil, and honey together in a bowl. Add chicken mixture, cherries, carrots, green onion, and almonds; toss to combine.
3. Spoon 1/12 the chicken/cherry mixture onto the center of each lettuce leaf; roll leaf around filling and serve.

PECAN SNACK
Servings: 32 | Prep: 10m | Cooks: 1h | Total: 1h10m

NUTRITION FACTS

Calories: 117| Carbohydrates: 6.7g | Fat: 10.2g | Protein: 1.4g | Cholesterol: 0mg

INGREDIENTS

- 1 egg white
- 1 tablespoon water
- 1 pound pecans

- 3/4 cup white sugar
- 1 teaspoon ground cinnamon
- 1 teaspoon salt

DIRECTIONS

1. Preheat oven to 250 degrees F (120 degrees C).
2. In a large bowl, beat egg white with water until frothy. Stir in pecans and mix to coat. Combine sugar, cinnamon and salt and stir into pecan mixture. Spread on a baking sheet.
3. Bake in preheated oven 1 hour, stirring every 15 minutes. Store in an airtight container.

THE BEST STUFFED MUSHROOMS

Servings: 8 | Prep: 10m | Cooks: 30m | Total: 40m

NUTRITION FACTS

Calories: 162 | Carbohydrates: 3.5g | Fat: 14g | Protein: 6.7g | Cholesterol: 33mg

INGREDIENTS

- 3 slices bacon
- 1/2 (8 ounce) package cream cheese, softened
- 2 tablespoons grated Parmesan cheese
- 3 drops Worcestershire sauce
- 2 dashes ground black pepper
- 1 pound mushrooms, stems removed
- 2 tablespoons grated Parmesan cheese

DIRECTIONS

1. Preheat an oven to 350 degrees F (175 degrees C).
2. Place the bacon in a large, deep skillet and cook over medium-high heat, turning occasionally, until crisp and evenly browned, about 10 minutes. Drain the bacon slices on a paper towel-lined plate; crumble the drained bacon into a bowl. Stir in the cream cheese, 2 tablespoons Parmesan cheese, Worcestershire sauce, and pepper until evenly mixed. Spoon the filling into the mushroom caps and place into an 8x8-inch baking dish. Sprinkle with the remaining 2 tablespoons of Parmesan cheese.
3. Bake in the preheated oven until the mushrooms are tender and the filling is golden brown, 25 to 30 minutes.

TORTILLA ROLLUPS

Servings: 20 | Prep: 20m | Cooks: 4h | Total: 4h20

NUTRITION FACTS

Calories: 176 | Carbohydrates: 19.3g | Fat: 8.6g | Protein: 5.3g | Cholesterol: 18mg

INGREDIENTS

- 1 (8 ounce) package cream cheese, softened
- 4 green onions, finely chopped
- 1/4 cup salsa
- 4 ounces shredded Cheddar cheese
- 10 (10 inch) flour tortillas

DIRECTIONS

1. In a medium bowl, mix together the cream cheese, green onions, salsa and Cheddar cheese.
2. Spread the cream cheese mixture on the tortillas. Roll the tortillas and refrigerate about 4 hours before slicing into 1 inch long pieces.

HOT SPINACH AND ARTICHOKE DIP

Servings: 48 | Prep: 10m | Cooks: 20m | Total: 30m

NUTRITION FACTS

Calories: 70 | Carbohydrates: 1.7g | Fat: 6.4g | Protein: 2.2g | Cholesterol: 9mg

INGREDIENTS

- 8 slices bacon
- 1 (10 ounce) package frozen chopped spinach, thawed and drained
- 1 (14 ounce) can quartered marinated artichoke hearts, drained
- 1 (5 ounce) container garlic-herb flavored cheese spread
- 1 cup grated Parmesan cheese
- 1 (8 ounce) container sour cream
- 1/2 cup mayonnaise

DIRECTIONS

1. Preheat oven to 400 degrees F (200 degrees C).
2. Place bacon in a large, deep skillet. Cook over medium high heat until evenly brown. Drain and crumble into a medium bowl.
3. Mix spinach, artichoke hearts, garlic-herb flavored cheese spread, Parmesan cheese, sour cream and mayonnaise into the bowl with bacon.
4. Scoop mixture into a 7x11 inch baking dish. Bake in the preheated oven 20 minutes, or until bubbly and lightly browned.

CRANBERRY DIP

Servings: 32 | Prep: 5m | Cooks: 20m | Total: 8h25m

NUTRITION FACTS

Calories: 103 | Carbohydrates: 14.7g | Fat: 5.2g | Protein: 1g | Cholesterol: 8mg

INGREDIENTS

- 1 (12 ounce) package fresh cranberries
- 1 cup white sugar
- 1 cup apricot jam
- 1 cup chopped pecans
- 1 (8 ounce) package cream cheese

DIRECTIONS

1. Preheat an oven to 350 degrees F (175 degrees C).
2. Combine cranberries with sugar in a 2 quart baking dish with a lid, stirring well to coat all the berries. Bake in the preheated oven, covered, for about 30 minutes, until the cranberries pop and release their liquid.
3. • Remove from oven and stir in the apricot jam and pecans. Refrigerate overnight to blend the flavors. To serve, allow the cream cheese to come to room temperature, and pour dip over the block of cream cheese on a serving dish. Serve with buttery round crackers or small pretzels.

SWEDISH MEATBALLS
Servings: 4 | Prep: 25m | Cooks: 30 | Total: 55m

NUTRITION FACTS

Calories: 906 | Carbohydrates: 29.6g | Fat: 70g | Protein: 38.5g | Cholesterol: 255mg

INGREDIENTS

- 6 tablespoons butter, divided
- 1 onion, chopped
- 1 cup dried bread crumbs
- 1 cup evaporated milk, divided
- 1 1/2 pounds ground beef
- 1 egg, beaten

- 1 teaspoon salt
- 1/4 teaspoon ground black pepper
- 1 pinch dried parsley
- 1 1/2 teaspoons all-purpose flour
- 1 tablespoon tomato sauce
- ground nutmeg to taste

DIRECTIONS

1. Melt 3 tablespoons butter in a large skillet over medium heat. Add the onion and saute for 5 to 10 minutes, or until tender.
2. In a separate bowl, combine the bread crumbs with 2 tablespoons of evaporated milk and stir, allowing the crumbs to absorb the milk. Add the ground beef, onion, egg, salt, ground black pepper and parsley to taste. Mix well and form into golf ball-sized meatballs.
3. Heat remaining butter in the same skillet over medium- to medium-high heat and add the meatballs. Carefully shake the skillet to turn the meatballs, as needed. Saute for 10 to 15 minutes, or until meatballs are browned on all sides. Transfer the meatballs to a serving platter, reserving the liquid in the skillet.
4. Add the flour to the skillet and stir until smooth. Then gradually add the evaporated milk, tomato sauce and nutmeg to taste; again stirring until mixture is warmed, smooth and creamy. Strain over meatballs.

SWEET AND GOOEY CHICKEN WINGS
Servings: 4 | Prep: 4h5m | Cooks: 1h35m | Total: 5h40m

NUTRITION FACTS

Calories: 464 | Carbohydrates: 16.2g | Fat: 28.9g | Protein: 33.3g | Cholesterol: 131mg

INGREDIENTS

- 1/2 cup soy sauce
- 1/4 cup packed brown sugar
- 1/2 tablespoon vegetable oil
- 1/2 teaspoon minced fresh ginger root
- 1/2 teaspoon garlic powder
- 1 1/2 pounds chicken wings

DIRECTIONS

1. In a 9x13 inch casserole, combine soy sauce, brown sugar, oil, ginger, and garlic powder. Mix until brown sugar completely dissolves into the mixture. Place the chicken wings in the dish and turn them over until they are all well coated. Cover the dish and refrigerate for at least 4 hours. Turn the chicken again, after 2 hours.
2. Preheat oven to 350 degrees F (175 degrees C).
3. Bake chicken at 350 degrees F (175 degrees C), covered, for 45 minutes. Turn the chicken wings, and spoon sauce from the bottom of the pan over the tops of the wings. Cook an additional 50 minutes, uncovered.

DOG FOOD DIP
Servings: 48 | Prep: 15m | Cooks: 20m | Total: 35m

NUTRITION FACTS

Calories: 88 | Carbohydrates: 1.5g | Fat: 6.6g | Protein: 5.3g | Cholesterol: 20mg

INGREDIENTS

- 2 pounds lean ground beef
- 1 onion, chopped
- 1 (10.75 ounce) can condensed cream of mushroom soup
- 1 pound processed cheese food, cubed
- pickled jalapeno pepper slices, to taste (optional)

DIRECTIONS

1. Place lean ground beef and onion in a large, deep skillet over medium high heat. Cook until beef is evenly brown and onion is soft. Drain and turn heat to medium low.
2. Pour in condensed cream of mushroom soup. Mix in processed cheese food and desired amount of jalapeno peppers. Cook and stir until all ingredients are well blended, about 10 minutes.
3. Transfer the mixture to a medium bowl. Cover and chill in the refrigerator 8 hours, or overnight.
4. Reheat the mixture in a slow cooker, mixing in about 1 tablespoon of water to thin if necessary, before serving.

CRAB CAKES
Servings: 5 | Prep: 45m | Cooks: 15m | Total: 1h

NUTRITION FACTS

Calories: 499 | Carbohydrates: 5.3g | Fat: 41.2g | Protein: 26.8g | Cholesterol: 142mg

INGREDIENTS

- 4 pounds crabmeat
- 1 egg
- 1 tablespoon lemon zest
- 1/8 teaspoon Old Bay Seasoning TM
- 3 egg yolks
- 1/8 teaspoon Old Bay Seasoning TM
- 3 ounces fresh lime juice

- 2 tablespoons fresh basil, chopped
- 1 cup saltine crackers, crushed
- 1 cup mayonnaise
- 4 tablespoons vegetable oil
- 2 tablespoons chopped fresh cilantro
- salt and pepper to taste
- 1 3/4 cups vegetable oil

DIRECTIONS

1. In a large mixing bowl, combine crabmeat, 1 egg, lemon zest, Old Bay Seasoning, chopped basil, crushed crackers and mayonnaise. Mix thoroughly.
2. Form 5 ounce patties out of the crab mixture (should make about 16 patties), and chill until cold before cooking.
3. In a skillet, heat 4 tablespoons of oil over medium heat. Saute the crab cakes for 4 minutes on each side or until golden brown.
4. For the sauce, in a blender place the egg yolks, Old Bay Seasoning, lime juice, cilantro, salt and pepper. Blend for 10 seconds. Keeping the blender running, slowly drizzle the oil into the blender. Blend until sauce is creamy.

AHI POKE BASIC
Servings: 4 | Prep: 15m | Cooks: 2h | Total: 2h15m

NUTRITION FACTS

Calories: 396 | Carbohydrates: 8.6g | Fat: 13.7g | Protein: 58.4g | Cholesterol: 102mg

INGREDIENTS

- 1 cup soy sauce
- 3/4 cup chopped green onions
- 1/4 cup chopped onion
- 1 tablespoon toasted sesame seeds
- 1 tablespoon crushed red pepper (optional)
- 2 tablespoons finely chopped macadamia nuts

DIRECTIONS

1. In a medium size non-reactive bowl, combine Ahi, soy sauce, green onions, sesame oil, sesame seeds, chili pepper, and macadamia nuts; mix well. Refrigerate at least 2 hours before serving.

WORLD'S BEST BACON CHEESE DIP
Servings: 16 | Prep: 15m | Cooks: 10m | Total: 25m

NUTRITION FACTS

Calories: 239 | Carbohydrates: 2.3g | Fat: 23.1g | Protein: 5.9g | Cholesterol: 38mg

INGREDIENTS

- 4 slices bacon
- 1 (8 ounce) package cream cheese, softened
- 1 cup mayonnaise
- 8 ounces Swiss cheese, shredded
- 2 green onions, finely chopped
- 4 buttery round crackers, crushed

DIRECTIONS

1. Place bacon in a large skillet. Cook over medium-high heat until evenly brown. Drain, crumble, and set aside.
2. In a small bowl, mix the cream cheese with mayonnaise until smooth. Stir in Swiss cheese, onions, and bacon. Place bowl in microwave, and cook 2 minutes. Remove, and stir well. Return to microwave, and cook 2 to 4 minutes more. Sprinkle crushed crackers on top. Serve warm with crackers.

SWEET COATED PECANS
Servings: 8 | Prep: 10m | Cooks: 1h | Total: 13h10m

NUTRITION FACTS

Calories: 492 | Carbohydrates: 33.1g | Fat: 40.8g | Protein: 5.7g | Cholesterol: 0mg

INGREDIENTS

- 1 egg white
- 1 teaspoon ground cinnamon
- 1 cup sugar
- 3/4 teaspoon salt
- 2 tablespoons water
- 1 pound pecan halves

DIRECTIONS

1. Preheat oven to 250 degrees F (120 degrees C). Lightly butter a baking sheet.
2. In a bowl, beat the egg white until foamy. Mix in cinnamon, sugar, salt, and water. Mix well. Stir in pecan halves, stirring until well coated. Spread on baking sheet.
3. Bake in preheated oven for 1 hour, stirring every 15 minutes.

DEEP FRIED JALAPENO SLICES

Servings: 8 | Prep: 5m | Cooks: 10m | Total: 15m

NUTRITION FACTS

Calories: 147 | Carbohydrates: 15g | Fat: 7.2g | Protein: 3.7g | Cholesterol: 46mg

INGREDIENTS

- 1 cup all-purpose flour
- 1 teaspoon salt
- 1 teaspoon ground black pepper
- 1 teaspoon chili powder
- 1 teaspoon garlic powder
- 2 eggs
- 1 cup beer
- 1/2 quart vegetable oil
- 2 cups sliced jalapeno peppers

DIRECTIONS

1. Mix flour, salt, pepper, red chili powder, garlic powder, eggs, and beer together in a bowl.
2. In a deep fryer, or large pot heat oil to 365 degrees F (180 degrees C).
3. Dip the sliced jalapenos in the batter. Place battered jalapenos in deep fryer. The jalapenos are fully cooked when they float to the surface of the oil. They should be golden brown and crispy. Enjoy!

ZUCCHINI CORN FRITTERS

Servings: 24 | Prep: 15m | Cooks: 4m | Total: 19m

NUTRITION FACTS

Calories: 144 | Carbohydrates: 15g | Fat: 8g | Protein: 3.6g | Cholesterol: 26mg

INGREDIENTS

- 2 cups all-purpose flour
- 1 tablespoon baking powder
- 1/2 teaspoon cumin
- 1/2 cup sugar
- 1/2 teaspoon salt
- fresh ground black pepper
- 2 eggs, beaten
- 1 cup milk
- 1/4 cup butter, melted
- 2 cups grated zucchini
- 1 1/2 cups fresh corn, kernels cut from cob
- 1 cup finely shredded Cheddar cheese
- oil for frying

DIRECTIONS

1. In a large bowl, stir together flour, baking powder, cumin, sugar, salt, and pepper.
2. In a small bowl, whisk together eggs, milk, and butter. Whisk wet ingredients into dry ingredients. Stir in zucchini, corn, and cheese; mix well.
3. Warm oil in a cast iron skillet over medium-high heat. Drop batter by the tablespoonful into hot oil. Fry until crisp and brown, turning once with tongs. Remove to paper towels.

ABSOLUTELY THE BEST NACHO DIP EVER
Servings: 6 | Prep: 30m | Cooks: 4h15 | Total: 4h45m

NUTRITION FACTS

Calories: 47 | Carbohydrates: 1.2g | Fat: 4.2g | Protein: 1.4g | Cholesterol: 9mg

INGREDIENTS

- 1 (8 ounce) package cream cheese, softened
- 1/2 cup sour cream
- 1/2 cup mayonnaise
- 1/4 cup cocktail sauce
- 1 cup mild salsa
- 3/4 cup diced green onion
- 3/4 cup diced red bell pepper
- 3/4 cup diced green bell pepper
- 2 cups shredded Cheddar cheese
- 2 cups shredded lettuce
- 1 cucumber, thinly sliced

DIRECTIONS

1. In a blender or food processor, thoroughly mix cream cheese, sour cream and mayonnaise. Spread the mixture evenly in the bottom of a medium serving dish.
2. In individual layers, top the mixture with cocktail sauce, mild salsa, diced green onion, red bell pepper, green bell pepper, shredded Cheddar cheese and shredded lettuce.
3. Arrange cucumber slices around the edge of the serving dish. Chill in the refrigerator at least 2 hours before serving.

AUTHENTIC MEXICAN SHRIMP COCKTAIL
Servings: 4 | Prep: 45m | Cooks: 1h | Total: 1h45

NUTRITION FACTS

Calories: 410 | Carbohydrates: 41.8g | Fat: 16.5g | Protein: 28.8g | Cholesterol: 221mg

INGREDIENTS

- 1/3 cup Spanish onion, chopped
- 1/4 cup freshly squeezed lime juice
- 1 pound chilled cooked medium shrimp - peeled, deveined, and tails removed
- 2 teaspoons salt
- 1 1/2 cups chilled tomato and clam juice cocktail (such as Clamato)
- 1 bunch fresh cilantro - stems discarded and leaves chopped
- 2 avocados - peeled, pitted, and chopped
- 2 roma (plum) tomatoes, chopped

- 1 cucumber, finely chopped
- 1 stalk celery, finely chopped
- 1 jalapeno pepper, seeded and finely chopped
- 2 teaspoons ground black pepper
- 1 cup chilled ketchup (such as Heinz)
- 2 tablespoons hot pepper sauce (such as Valentina)

DIRECTIONS

1. Mix onion with lime juice in a small bowl and allow to stand for 10 minutes. Meanwhile, toss shrimp, roma tomatoes, cucumber, celery, jalapeno, salt, and black pepper in a bowl until thoroughly combined.
2. Whisk tomato and clam juice cocktail, ketchup, cilantro, and hot pepper sauce in a separate bowl; stir dressing into shrimp mixture. Gently fold in avocados. Cover and chill thoroughly, at least 1 hour.

CANDIED BACON
Servings: 6 | Prep: 5m | Cooks: 50m | Total: 55m

NUTRITION FACTS

Calories: 187 | Carbohydrates: 13.9g | Fat: 10.4g | Protein: 9.2g | Cholesterol: 27mg

INGREDIENTS

- 1/4 cup packed brown sugar
- 2 tablespoons rice vinegar
- 2 tablespoons maple syrup
- ground black pepper to taste
- 1 pound thick-cut bacon

DIRECTIONS

1. Preheat oven to 350 degrees F (175 degrees C).
2. Mix brown sugar, rice vinegar, maple syrup, and black pepper in a small bowl.
3. Place bacon slices on cooling rack set over a baking sheet.
4. Bake in the preheated oven for 10 minutes, turn slices, and bake another 5 minutes.
5. Remove bacon and brush both sides with brown sugar mixture. Return bacon to the oven and bake another 5 minutes. Repeat basting every 5 minutes until bacon is browned and crisp, about 35 minutes.

SWEET AND SOUR MEATBALLS

Servings: 16 | Prep: 15m | Cooks: m | Total: 50m

NUTRITION FACTS

Calories: 357 | Carbohydrates: 34.9g | Fat: 15.2g | Protein: 19.8g | Cholesterol: 95mg

INGREDIENTS

- 1 (16 ounce) can sauerkraut
- 1 (16 ounce) can jellied cranberry sauce
- 1/2 cup packed brown sugar
- 1/2 (16 ounce) jar spaghetti sauce
- 3 pounds small meatballs

DIRECTIONS

1. In a medium bowl, mix sauerkraut, jellied cranberry sauce, brown sugar and spaghetti sauce.
2. Place meatballs in a slow cooker set to low. Cover with the sauerkraut mixture. Cook 3 to 4 hours, stirring occasionally.

SWEET PARTY MIX

Servings: 24 | Prep: 15m | Cooks: 1h | Total: 1h15

NUTRITION FACTS

Calories: 267 | Carbohydrates: 35.6g | Fat: 13.9g | Protein: 3g | Cholesterol: 15mg

INGREDIENTS

- 1 (12 ounce) package crispy corn and rice cereal
- 5 ounces slivered almonds
- 6 ounces toasted, chopped pecans
- 3/4 cup butter
- 3/4 cup dark corn syrup
- 1 1/2 cups light brown sugar

DIRECTIONS

1. Preheat oven to 250 degrees F (120 degrees C). Lightly grease a large roasting pan.
2. In a large bowl, mix crispy corn and rice cereal, slivered almonds and toasted, chopped pecans.
3. In a medium saucepan over medium heat, melt the butter and mix with dark corn syrup and light brown sugar. Pour the mixture over the crispy corn and rice cereal mixture. Stir and shake to coat all the nuts and cereal.
4. Pour the coated mixture into the prepared roasting pan. Stirring approximately every 15 minutes, cook 1 hour in the preheated oven. Cool on wax paper, and store in airtight containers.

CRISPY CHICKEN STRIPS
Servings: 4 | Prep: 15m | Cooks: 25m | Total: 40m

NUTRITION FACTS

Calories: 280 | Carbohydrates: 12g | Fat: 14.4g | Protein: 24.8g | Cholesterol: 95mg

INGREDIENTS

- 1/4 cup butter, melted
- 1 1/2 cups crispy rice cereal, coarsely crushed
- 2 tablespoons all-purpose flour
- 2 teaspoons salt-free seasoning blend
- 1 pound boneless, skinless chicken breast tenders

DIRECTIONS

1. Preheat oven to 400 degrees F (200 degrees C). Lightly grease a 9x13 inch baking dish.

2. Place butter in a shallow bowl. In a separate shallow bowl, mix the crushed cereal, flour, and seasoning blend. Dip chicken tenders in the butter, then press in the cereal mixture to evenly coat. Arrange in the prepared baking dish. Drizzle with any remaining butter.

3. Bake 25 minutes in the preheated oven, or until chicken juices run clear.

STUFFED CREAM CHEESE MUSHROOMS

Servings: 6 | Prep: 15m | Cooks: 25m | Total: 40m

NUTRITION FACTS

Calories: 176 | Carbohydrates: 2.9g | Fat: 16.4g | Protein: 5.3g | Cholesterol: 44mg

INGREDIENTS

- 1 serving cooking spray
- 12 whole fresh mushrooms, tough ends trimmed
- 12 whole fresh mushrooms, tough ends trimmed
- 1 tablespoon vegetable oil
- 1/4 teaspoon onion powder
- 1 tablespoon minced garlic
- 1 (8 ounce) package cream cheese, softened
- 1/4 cup grated Parmesan cheese
- 1/4 teaspoon ground black pepper
- 1/4 teaspoon cayenne pepper

DIRECTIONS

1. Preheat oven to 350 degrees F (175 degrees C). Prepare a baking sheet with cooking spray.
2. Clean mushrooms with a damp paper towel. Carefully break stems from mushrooms. Chop stems extremely fine.
3. Heat oil in a large skillet over medium heat. Fry chopped mushroom stems and garlic in hot oil until any moisture has disappeared, taking care not to burn the garlic, 3 to 5 minutes. Spread mushroom mixture into a bowl to cool completely, about 10 minutes.
4. Stir cream cheese, Parmesan cheese, black pepper, onion powder, and cayenne pepper with the mushroom stems and garlic until very thick and completely mixed. Use a small spoon fill each mushroom cap with a generous amount of stuffing. Arrange stuffed mushrooms onto the prepared cookie sheet.
5. Bake in preheated oven until piping hot and liquid starts to form under the caps, about 20 minutes.

MAKING CRISPY ONION RINGS

Servings: 8 | Prep: 10m | Cooks: 20m | Total: 30m

NUTRITION FACTS

Calories: 179 | Carbohydrates: 7.1g | Fat: 6.5g | Protein: 4.1g | Cholesterol: 0mg

INGREDIENTS

- 1/2 cup all-purpose flour
- 1/4 cup cornstarch
- 1/8 teaspoon cayenne pepper, or to taste
- 1 cup chilled club soda

- 2 tablespoons dry potato flakes
- 2 cups vegetable oil for frying
- fine salt to taste

- 2 cups panko bread crumbs, or as needed
- 2 large onions, cut into 1/4-inch thick slices and separated into rings
-

DIRECTIONS

1. Whisk together flour, cornstarch, dry potato flakes, and cayenne pepper in a large bowl. Whisk in club soda to make a smooth batter.
2. Place panko bread crumbs in a shallow bowl.
3. Heat oil in a deep fryer or large saucepan to 350 degrees F (175 degrees C).
4. Place a few onion rings at a time into the bowl of batter and turn to coat all sides with batter.
5. Remove onion rings from batter and place into pan of panko bread crumbs; turn to coat completely with crumbs.
6. Cook a few rings at a time in the hot oil until golden brown, about 2 to 3 minutes.
7. Transfer to a cooling rack set over paper towels to drain. Season with salt to taste and serve.

STEF'S SUPER CHEESY GARLIC BREAD
Servings: 8 | Prep: 10m | Cooks: 10h | Total: 20m

NUTRITION FACTS

Calories: 555 | Carbohydrates: 25.4g | Fat: 39g | Protein: 17.5g | Cholesterol: 68mg

INGREDIENTS

- 1/2 cup butter, softened
- 3/4 cup mayonnaise
- 1 bunch green onions, chopped
- 3 cloves garlic, minced

- 1 1/4 cups Parmesan cheese
- 1 1/2 cups shredded Monterey Jack cheese
- 1 (1 pound) loaf French bread, halved lengthwise

DIRECTIONS

1. Preheat an oven to 350 degrees F (175 degrees C).
2. Combine the butter, mayonnaise, green onions, garlic, Parmesan cheese, and Monterey Jack cheese in a large bowl. Cut each half of French bread into 4 pieces. Spread the cheese mixture evenly on the bread pieces.
3. Bake in the preheated oven for 8 minutes. Set the oven to broil; broil until hot and bubbly, about 2 additional minutes.

SPAM MUSUBI

Servings: 10 | Prep: 25m | Cooks: 30m | Total: 5h25m | Additional: 4h30m

NUTRITION FACTS

Calories: 276 | Carbohydrates: 34.7g | Fat: 12g | Protein: 6.8g | Cholesterol: 24mg

INGREDIENTS

- 2 cups uncooked short-grain white rice
- 2 cups water
- 6 tablespoons rice vinegar
- 1/4 cup soy sauce
- 2 tablespoons vegetable oil

- 1/4 cup oyster saucetomatoes, undrained
- 1/2 cup white sugar
- 1 (12 ounce) container fully cooked luncheon meat (e.g. Spam)
- 5 sheets sushi nori (dry seaweed)
-

DIRECTIONS

1. Soak uncooked rice for 4 hours; drain and rinse.
2. In a saucepan bring 2 cups water to a boil. Add rice and stir. Reduce heat, cover, and simmer for 20 minutes. Stir in rice vinegar, and set aside to cool.
3. In a separate bowl, stir together soy sauce, oyster sauce, and sugar until sugar is completely dissolved. Slice luncheon meat lengthwise into 10 slices, or to desired thickness, and marinate in sauce for 5 minutes
4. In a large skillet, heat oil over medium high heat. Cook slices for 2 minutes per side, or until lightly browned. Cut nori sheets in half and lay on a flat work surface. Place a rice press in the center of the sheet, and press rice tightly inside. Top with a slice of luncheon meat, and remove press. Wrap nori around rice mold, sealing edges with a small amount of water. (Rice may also be formed by hand in the shape of the meat slices, 1 inch thick.) Musubi may be served warm or chilled.

EASY BUTTERNUT SQUASH RAVIOLI

Servings: 6 | Prep: 30m | Cooks: 10m | Total: 40m

NUTRITION FACTS

Calories: 378 | Carbohydrates: 47.4g | Fat: 15.9g | Protein: 11.5g | Cholesterol: 79mg

INGREDIENTS

- 1 cup mashed, cooked butternut squash
- 1 egg yolk

- 1/2 teaspoon salt
- 1/2 teaspoon freshly ground black pepper
- 1 pinch cayenne pepper
- 1/2 cup mascarpone cheese
- chopped fresh sage to taste
- 1/3 cup grated Parmesan cheese
- 1 (16 ounce) package round wonton wrappers
- 2 tablespoons butter
- 1 clove garlic, unpeeled
- 1 tablespoon grated Parmesan cheese, or to taste

DIRECTIONS

1. Place cooked squash into a mixing bowl. Add salt, black pepper, and cayenne pepper. Stir in mascarpone cheese, egg yolk, and 1/3 cup Parmesan cheese, mixing until the filling is smoothly combined.
2. Place a wonton wrapper onto a working surface. Wet the tip of a finger in water, and run it all along the outer edge of the wonton skin to moisten. Place about 1 teaspoon of filling in the center of the wonton. Fold the wonton in half to make a half-moon shape, and press the edges to seal. Repeat with the remaining wonton wrappers.
3. Place a deep skillet over medium-low heat. Stir in butter and unpeeled clove of garlic. Meanwhile, bring a saucepan of lightly salted water to a boil.
4. Drop the filled raviolis into the boiling water, a few at a time, and cook until they float to the top, about 2 minutes. Drain the raviolis, and transfer them to the skillet. Turn the heat under the skillet up to medium-high, and cook just until the raviolis are infused with garlic flavor, about 2 or 3 more minutes. Sprinkle with chopped sage, more black pepper, and extra Parmesan cheese to taste.

MEXICAN POTATO NACHOS
Servings: 8 | Prep: 20m | Cooks: 40m | Total: 1h

NUTRITION FACTS

Calories: 327 | Carbohydrates: 20g | Fat: 18.6g | Protein: 16.4g | Cholesterol: 50mg

INGREDIENTS

- 2 tablespoons Vegetable oil
- 2 large baking potatoes, cut into 1/2-inch thick slices
- salt and ground black pepper to taste
- 1 tablespoon vegetable oil
- 8 ounces shredded Cheddar cheese, divided
- 1 small tomato, chopped
- 1/2 pound ground beef
- 1 (15 ounce) can black beans, drained
- 2 tablespoons taco seasoning
- 2 tablespoons water
- 1/4 cup shredded lettuce
- 1/4 cup sour cream

- 1/4 cup guacamole

DIRECTIONS

1. Preheat oven to 450 degrees F (230 degrees C).
2. Pour 2 tablespoons of vegetable oil into a large bowl; toss the potato slices in the oil to coat.
3. Arrange the slices in a single layer on a baking sheet and sprinkle with salt and black pepper.
4. Bake in the preheated oven until the potato slices are golden brown, about 20 minutes.
5. While potato slices are baking, heat 1 tablespoon of vegetable oil in a skillet over medium heat; brown the ground beef in the hot oil, breaking it up into crumbles as it cooks, 8 to 10 minutes. Drain excess grease.
6. Mix the black beans into the ground beef; stir in the taco seasoning and water. Bring the mixture to a boil and reduce heat to medium-low. Simmer until the flavors have blended, about 10 minutes.
7. Arrange the potato slices on a serving platter and sprinkle with half the Cheddar cheese.
8. Top the potatoes with the meat and bean mixture; sprinkle the remaining cheese on the nachos.
9. Spread the lettuce out over the nachos and garnish with tomato and dollops of sour cream and guacamole.

SWEET CHILI THAI SAUCE
Servings: 24 | Prep: 15m | Cooks: 5m | Total: 20m

NUTRITION FACTS

Calories: 24 | Carbohydrates: 8.7g | Fat: 0g | Protein: 0g | Cholesterol: 0mg

INGREDIENTS

- 1 cup water

- 1 cup rice vinegar

- 1 cup sugar

- 2 teaspoons cornstarch

- 1 teaspoon garlic, minced

- 2 teaspoons hot chile pepper, minced

- 2 teaspoons ketchup

DIRECTIONS

1. Pour water and vinegar into a saucepan, and bring to a boil over high heat. Stir in sugar, ginger, garlic, chile pepper, and ketchup; simmer for 5 minutes. Stir in cornstarch. Remove saucepan from stove to cool. Then transfer to a bowl, cover, and refrigerate until needed.

DOUBLE CHILI CHEESE DIP
Servings: 12 | Prep: 5m | Cooks: 20m | Total: 25m

Calories: 134 | Carbohydrates: 3.8g | Fat: 10.6g | Protein: 6.4g | Cholesterol: 36mg

INGREDIENTS

- 1 (8 ounce) package cream cheese, softened
- 1 (15 ounce) can chili without beans
- 4 green onions, thinly sliced
- 1/4 cup diced green chiles, drained
- 1 cup shredded Cheddar cheese

DIRECTIONS

1. Preheat oven to 350 degrees F (175 degrees C). Grease a 9-inch pie plate.
2. Spread cream cheese into the prepared pie plate. Top the cream cheese with chili, onions, chilies, and cheese.
3. Bake at 350 degrees F (175 degrees C) for 15 to 20 minutes.

HOT SPINACH ARTICHOKE DIP

Servings: 6 | Prep: 15m | Cooks: 30m | Total: 45m

NUTRITION FACTS

Calories: 284 | Carbohydrates: 8.8g | Fat: 22.9g | Protein: 12.7g | Cholesterol: 71mg

INGREDIENTS

- 2 tablespoons butter
- 1/2 cup green onions, white and light green parts only, thinly sliced
- 2 cloves garlic, minced
- salt
- 1 (14 ounce) can artichoke hearts, drained and chopped
- 1 (10 ounce) package frozen chopped spinach , thawed, drained and squeezed dry
- 1/4 cup shredded mozzarella cheese
- 8 ounces cream cheese
- 1/2 cup shredded Gruyere cheese
- 1/2 cup finely grated Parmigiano-Reggiano cheese
- 1/4 teaspoon hot sauce
- 1 pinch ground nutmeg
- salt and freshly ground black pepper to taste

DIRECTIONS

1. Preheat oven to 400 degrees F (200 degrees C).

2. Melt butter in a saucepan over medium-low heat; stir in onions and pinch of salt. Cook, stirring occasionally, until onions are soft, about 5 minutes. Stir garlic into onions and remove from heat.
3. Mix green onion mixture, spinach, artichoke hearts, cream cheese, Gruyere, Parmigiano-Reggiano, hot sauce, nutmeg, salt, and pepper in a large bowl until combined.
4. Spoon artichoke mixture into two ramekins. Top each with shredded mozzarella cheese.
5. Bake in the preheated oven until tops are golden brown and bubbling, about 25 minutes.

EASY CHICKEN TAQUITOS
Servings: 6 | Prep: 15m | Cooks: 30m | Total: 45m

NUTRITION FACTS

Calories: 209 | Carbohydrates: 23.3g | Fat: 6.8g | Protein: 14.3g | Cholesterol: 34mg

INGREDIENTS

- 1 (10 ounce) can chicken chunks, drained
- 1/4 cup shredded Cheddar cheese
- 5 drops hot pepper sauce (such as Tabasco®)
- 12 corn tortillas

DIRECTIONS

1. Preheat an oven to 350 degrees F (175 degrees C). Lightly grease a 9x13 inch baking dish.
2. Combine the chicken and cheese in a bowl; stir in the hot pepper sauce. Warm the tortillas one at a time in a skillet over medium heat until flexible about 10 seconds per side.
3. Spread about 1 heaping tablespoon of the chicken over half of the warmed tortilla. Roll tightly to form the taquito starting at the filled side of the tortilla. Place seamed side down in the baking dish. Repeat with the remaining tortillas. Bake for 30 minutes in the preheated oven.

BACON CHEDDAR JALAPENO POPPERS
Servings: 12 | Prep: 10m | Cooks: 10m | Total: 20m

NUTRITION FACTS

Calories: 281 | Carbohydrates: 1.1g | Fat: 25g | Protein: 12.6g | Cholesterol: 58mg

INGREDIENTS

- 1 (16 ounce) package Cheddar cheese
- 6 jalapeno peppers, seeded and halved
- 12 slices bacon

DIRECTIONS

1. Preheat the broiler.
2. Cut Cheddar cheese into 12 slices long enough to fit inside the jalapeno halves. Insert cheese slices into the halves. Wrap the jalapeno halves with the bacon slices, securing with a toothpick, if necessary. Place on a medium baking sheet.
3. Broil 5 to 10 minutes, or until the bacon is evenly brown.

SIMPLE ARTICHOKE DIP
Servings: 7 | Prep: 5m | Cooks: 20m | Total: 25m

NUTRITION FACTS

Calories: 293 | Carbohydrates: 5.1g | Fat: 28.2g | Protein: 5.9g | Cholesterol: 22mg

INGREDIENTS

- 1 (14 ounce) can artichoke hearts, drained and chopped
- 1 cup mayonnaise

- 1 cup grated Parmesan cheese

DIRECTIONS

1. Preheat oven to 375 degrees F (190 degrees C).
2. Combine the artichoke hearts, mayonnaise and Parmesan cheese and mix well. Spread mixture in a 9x13-inch baking dish and bake in the preheated oven for 15 to 20 minutes, or until bubbly and golden brown.

GARLIC BREAD
Servings: 15 | Prep: 5m | Cooks: 3h | Total: 3h5m

NUTRITION FACTS

Calories: 175 | Carbohydrates: 29.7g | Fat: 3.7g | Protein: 5.2g | Cholesterol: 1mg

INGREDIENTS

- 1 3/8 cups water
- 3 tablespoons olive oil
- 1 teaspoon minced garlic
- 4 cups bread flour
- 3 tablespoons white sugar
- 1 teaspoon coarsely ground black pepper

- 2 teaspoons salt
- 1/4 cup grated Parmesan cheese
- 1 teaspoon dried basil
- 1 teaspoon garlic powder
- 3 tablespoons chopped fresh chives
- 2 1/2 teaspoons bread machine yeast

DIRECTIONS

1. Place ingredients in the bread machine pan in the order suggested by the manufacturer.
2. Select Basic or White Bread cycle, and press Start.

HALLOWEEN EYE OF NEWT
Servings: 12 | Prep: 10m | Cooks: 15m | Total:25m

NUTRITION FACTS

Calories: 99 | Carbohydrates: 1.8g | Fat: 7.5g | Protein: 6.5g | Cholesterol: 186mg

INGREDIENTS

- 12 eggs
- 1 tablespoon sweet pickle relish
- 1 tablespoon mayonnaise
- 1 pinch celery salt
- 1 tablespoon prepared yellow mustard
- 2 drops green food coloring, or as needed
- 1 (6 ounce) can sliced black olives, drained

DIRECTIONS

1. Place all of the eggs into a large pot so they can rest on the bottom in a single layer. Fill with just enough cold water to cover the eggs. Bring to a boil, then cover, remove from the heat and let stand for about 15 minutes. Rinse under cold water or add some ice to the water and let the eggs cool completely. Peel and slice in half lengthwise.
2. Remove the yolks from the eggs and place them in a bowl. Mix in the relish, mayonnaise, celery salt, mustard, and food coloring. Spoon this filling into the egg whites and place them on a serving tray. Round the top of the filling using the spoon. Place an olive slice on each yolk to create the center of the eye. Dab a tiny bit of mayonnaise in the center of the olive as a finishing touch.

RED POTATO BITES
Servings: 40 | Prep: 15m | Cooks: 20m | Total: 45m

NUTRITION FACTS

Calories: 36 | Carbohydrates: 3g | Fat: 2.2g | Protein: 1.3g | Cholesterol: 5mg

INGREDIENTS

- 1 1/2 pounds small round red potatoes
- 1 tablespoon chopped fresh chives

- 4 slices bacon
- 1 cup sour cream
- 1/2 teaspoon seasoned salt
- 1/2 cup shredded Cheddar cheese
- parsley
- 1/4 teaspoon black pepper

DIRECTIONS

1. Preheat the oven to 375 degrees F (190 degrees C). Place potatoes in a saucepan, and add enough water to cover. Bring to boil, and cook until tender but still firm, about 10 minutes. Drain, and cool in a bowl of cold water.

2. Cook bacon in a skillet over medium-high heat until evenly browned. Drain, crumble, and set aside.
3. Remove cooled potatoes from water. Pat dry with a paper towel, and cut in half. Using a small spoon, carefully remove a small amount from center, leaving approximately 1/4 inch rim around each potato. Set reserved potato aside.
4. In a bowl, mix together reserved potato, sour cream, bacon, seasoned salt, pepper, and chives. Spoon a small amount of mixture into each potato half and place on a baking sheet. Top each potato off with some shredded cheese.
5. Bake for 10 minutes in the preheated oven, or until cheese is melted and potatoes are warmed through. Garnish with parsley, and serve.

Made in the USA
Monee, IL
20 November 2020